THE ART OF FRESHWATER FISHING

THE HUNTING & FISHING LIBRARY

Golden Press · New York

Western Publishing Company, Inc.

Racine, Wisconsin

By Dick Sternberg

DICK STERNBERG blends his years of angling experience and scientific training into a text loaded with important facts about fish and helpful tips for the modern
angler. A professional fisheries biologist for 16 years,
Dick has fished from the mountain streams of Alaska to
the Everglades of Florida. His articles have appeared in
numerous regional and national outdoor magazines.

CREDITS:
Project Director and Author: Dick Sternberg
Editorial Director: Chuck Wechsler
Design and Production: Cy DeCosse Creative Department, Inc.
Art Directors: Cy DeCosse, Delores Swanson
Production Coordinators: Bernice Maehren, Christine Watkins
Staff Photographers: Graham Brown, Buck Holzemer, Michael Jensen
Contributing Photographers: Larry Alvar, Art Carter, Elgin Ciampi,
   Cy DeCosse, Michael DeCosse, Dr. Calvin Fremling, Dan Gapen,
   Joe Geis, Michael Groppoli, Steve Grooms, Jane Harper, Merlyn
   Hilmoe, David Kumlein, Dr. Robert Megard, Steven McHugh,
   Doug Stamm, Jerry Stebbins, Dick Sternberg, Chuck Wechsler,
   Tom Zenanko
Photography Sources: Berkley and Company, Inc.; Eros Data Center;
   In-Fisherman Magazine; Minnesota Department of Natural
   Resources; Montana Department of Fish, Wildlife and Parks;
   Nebraska Game and Parks Commission; Steinhart Aquarium
Contributing Writers: Tom Cwynar, Craig Fisk, Steve Grooms,
   Chet Meyers, Tom Osborn, Jim Schneider, Don Woods
Illustrator: Ron Johnson
Typesetter: Jennie Smith
Consultants: Bud Burger, Ted Burger, Steve Grooms, Jim Maus,
   Ron Schara
Cooperating Agencies and Individuals: Alumacraft Boat Company;
   Max Bachhuber, Bantas Fishing Float; Paul C. Johnson, Berkley and
   Company Inc.; Burger Brothers Sporting Goods; Dr. Dwight
   Burkhardt, University of Minnesota; Lee Eberle and Ken Mueller,
   Northern States Power Company; Fenwick/Woodstream;
   In-Fisherman Magazine; Minnesota Department of Natural
   Resources; Frank Schneider, Jr., Muskies, Inc; John Schneider
Color Separations: Weston Engraving Co., Inc.
Printing: Moebius Printing Co.

Produced in the U.S.A.
Library of Congress Catalog Card Number:
 82-80787
Golden® and Golden Press® are trademarks of
 Western Publishing Company, Inc.
ISBN 0-307-46630-2

Contents

Introduction

The world of freshwater fishing is rapidly changing. Modern technology has created a wide array of sophisticated electronic equipment to help us find fish quickly. Super-light rods made of space-age materials help us detect bites more easily. We can buy better boats and motors, lines that are nearly invisible, and lures that closely resemble real baitfish. Even hooks and sinkers are greatly improved.

Today, the fresh waters of North America hold more gamefish than at any other time in history. Construction of thousands of reservoirs and millions of small ponds has turned desert and farmland into some of the most productive fishing waters on the continent. Modern fish management techniques have made it possible to enhance native fish populations and to introduce new species, such as sea-run salmon and striped bass, in freshwater lakes and reservoirs. The up-to-date range maps in this book show the many new fishing areas created by advanced stocking methods.

Despite the modern innovations in equipment, new fish species and millions of acres of new waters, many anglers are not broadening their fishing horizons. Instead, they continue to fish the same waters the same way they always have. And, if their favorite methods fail, they go home skunked. No wonder that a surprisingly small percentage of fishermen catch the vast majority of fish.

This book is intended to help anglers break the *one-species, one-method* habit. It presents the proven techniques for catching the most popular gamefish in virtually every type of water in North America. It also focuses on fish behavior and habitat, two areas where even experienced anglers can benefit by expanding their knowledge.

These pages reflect the combined experience of expert fishermen, biologists, outdoor writers and underwater photographers. Whenever possible, color photographs tell the story.

Among the book's 460 pictures are dozens of above-water scenes of lakes and streams matched with below-water glimpses of fish in their natural habitat. High-altitude NASA photographs show the prominent features of lakes, rivers and reservoirs, while scanning electron microscope photos magnify fishing lines up to 400 times actual size. Life-size closeups feature the proven lures for each gamefish. Multiple-exposure photos track the action of artificial lures. Hundreds of other photographs show the latest fishing equipment and techniques, along with step-by-step procedures for tying the most popular and successful fishing rigs.

Versatility, the underlying theme of this book, is the secret to becoming a better fisherman. Dozens of factors constantly influence where fish are found, what they eat and the mood they are in. An angler must be prepared to reach into his bag of tricks, come up with the technique best-suited to the conditions at hand, and have *confidence* in his angling strategy. Reading this book and studying its photographs is the first step toward developing this versatility. The rest is up to you.

All About Fish

The Senses of Fish

Fish are fine-tuned to their watery world. They have the same senses as other animals: sight, hearing, taste, smell and touch. In addition, fish have a unique sense, the lateral line, which enables them to find food and detect danger even when they are unable to see.

LATERAL LINE. Nerve endings along each side of the fish sense vibrations in the water, helping fish to determine the shape, speed, action and direction of objects. Small fish, such as perch and bluegills, use this sense to escape predators, darting into small crevices in rocks or gaps in thick weeds. Pike, walleyes, bass, large trout and other predators rely on the lateral line to pursue speeding baitfish unerringly. The lateral line also helps fish to swim smoothly in compact schools.

SIGHT. Like humans, fish see brightness and color by means of rods and cones in the retina. Rods sense light intensity, while cones identify light and color.

Many shallow-water fish such as bass have excellent color vision. In bright light near the surface, these species can detect most of the colors seen by the human eye. But many fish cannot see the full range of colors. Walleyes, for example, see only orange and green. Other colors appear as shades of gray.

Water filters out color, so fish in deep water cannot see the spectrum of colors that is visible at the surface. Red is the first to disappear, yellow is next and blue is last. Because they see little or no color in the depths, fish respond instead to flashes of light reflected off predators or prey. The eyes of some fish, however, are super-sensitive to certain colors, even in deep water. Green and especially orange, for example, are visible to walleyes at depths where humans would see no color at all.

Although most gamefish have color vision, a lure's color and pattern often means less to fish than its brightness and action. This probably explains why red-and-white spoons, yellow pork rind and purple worms catch fish, even though these colors are unnatural to fish. There are times, however, when a lure must be an exact imitation of the fish's natural foods. An example is when trout are feeding on a certain insect, while ignoring all others.

The distance fish can see under water depends on water clarity. Some gamefish can see 100 feet or more in very clear water, though a more likely range for lake-dwelling fish is 10 to 20 feet.

Fish view the outside world through a *window* in the water surface. The diameter of the window is about twice as wide as the fish is deep. In other words, a fish 5 feet below the surface would have a window 10 feet in diameter. Because of the way light rays bend when entering the water, fish can see objects above water that are far to the side of the window. Surrounding the window is the *mirror,* a large area of water surface through which fish cannot see. Images of underwater objects are mirrored on the underside of the surface film.

HEARING. Fish have a keen sense of hearing, partly because water conducts sound better than air. They lack external ears, but pick up sound directly through the bones of the head. Response to sound varies greatly from species to species. Although a light step on the bank might spook a trout, no

THE LATERAL LINE is a row of pores along the midline, extending from just behind the gill to the tail. Just beneath the line is a nerve with tiny branches that protrude through the pores. These nerve endings pick up vibrations and transmit them to the inner ear. The lateral line may be as important to a fish's survival as its eyes.

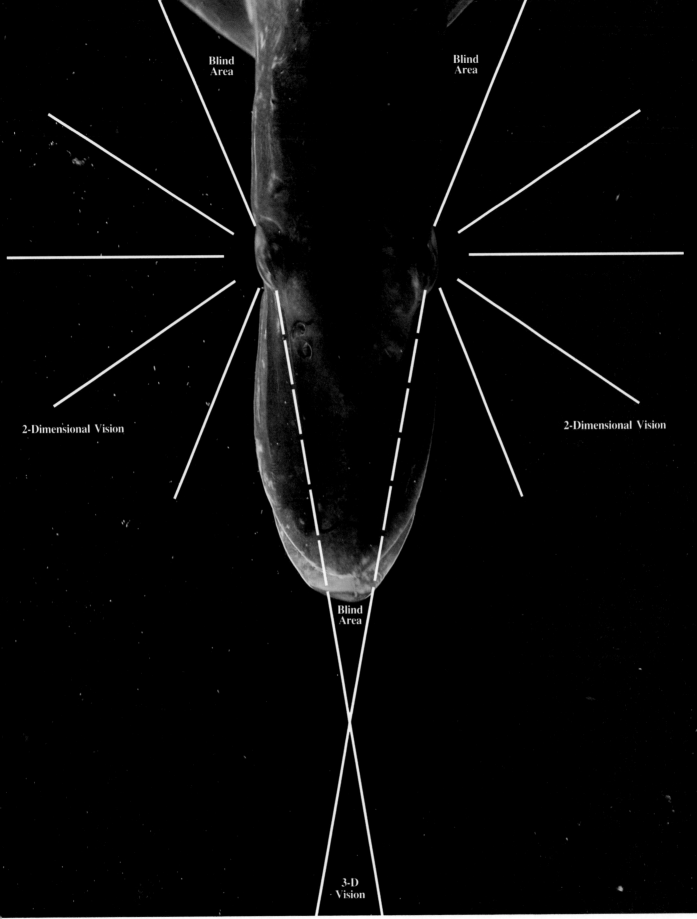

Blind Area

Blind Area

2-Dimensional Vision

2-Dimensional Vision

Blind Area

3-D Vision

EYE PLACEMENT gives fish a wide field of vision. They can see in all directions except straight down and straight back. To judge distance, a fish must turn to view the object with both eyes. Depth perception is possible in the triangle (indicated). Pike have sighting grooves that widen their field of three-dimensional vision.

reasonable amount of noise on a dock seems to disturb a sunfish; it may even attract them.

TASTE. Most fish can detect taste to some degree, though few species rely primarily on taste to find and identify food. Notable exceptions are bullheads and catfish. Their skin and especially their barbels or whiskers have taste-sensitive cells that enable them to test food before eating it.

SMELL. Fish detect smell with great sensitivity. Salmon, hundreds of miles at sea, return to spawn by tracking the odor of water from home streams. Some fish smell certain substances in concentrations as low as a few parts per trillion. This is roughly equivalent to one eyedropper of a substance in a 200-acre lake 20 feet deep.

Smell also alerts fish to the presence of predators or prey. When attacked by a predator, a baitfish emits a chemical from its skin that warns other baitfish to flee. Salmon and trout on a spawning run will retreat downstream if the skin of a human or bear comes in contact with the water. In one laboratory experiment, when a small amount of water from a tank containing northern pike was put into a tank with perch, the perch became terrified. Predators

SOUND produced by a lure may attract fish, especially in murky water. Some lures have rattles or internal beads that make noise when pulled through the water.

THE WINDOW is the round area at the surface through which fish view the outside world. The diameter of the window is about twice the depth of the fish.

THE LENS from a fish's eye offers a different look at the underwater world. The wide angle of vision gives rise to a namesake: the fish-eye lens used in photography.

such as pike, muskies and walleyes can distinguish smells of live or dead baitfish.

TOUCH. Fish are cold-blooded, which means their body temperature is the same as their environment. Nerves in their skin can detect temperature changes as small as one-tenth of one degree. Most species have a well-developed sense of touch. A bass will mouth a soft, plastic jig longer than a bucktail or feather jig, giving the angler more time to set the hook. Evidently, the soft plastic feels like real food.

Anglers can catch more fish by understanding the senses of gamefish and adjusting their activities and equipment accordingly. For example, when experimenting to find the right color of lure, walleye fishermen try fluorescent orange because they know walleyes see orange best. Trout fishermen, understanding the concept of the fish's window, stay low when approaching the streambank. And, knowing that the trout's lateral line senses vibrations, they take care to step lightly. Catfish anglers, knowing that channel cats are attracted by taste and smell, use stinkbaits, the smellier the better. Salmon fishermen, knowing that coho and chinook prefer water of 55°F, use underwater thermometers to locate the best fishing depth.

AT NIGHT, fish can easily see shallow-running lures against the lighter-colored surface. They have trouble seeing deep-running lures against the bottom.

SMELL is detected by the nasal sac inside the snout. Water is drawn into a front opening or *nare,* passed through the nasal sac and expelled through a back nare.

OILS AND GELS appeal to the fish's sense of smell. They are applied to plastic worms, plugs and live bait. Catfish anglers use stinkbaits, cheese and dried blood.

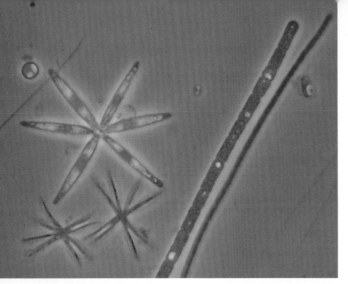

ALGAE are tiny plants that form the foundation of the aquatic food chain. A high-power microscope reveals a fascinating array of different shapes and patterns among various species of algae.

Food

Fish learn by trial and error what is edible and what is not. Young fish approach unfamiliar food with caution and often eject the morsel several times before swallowing it. But once they learn what is acceptable, they become much less cautious about eating similar items.

Over the years, fish build up a long list of acceptable foods and among these, a set of preferred items. However, many of their favorite foods, such as insects, are usually available for only brief periods. At other times, fish cannot afford to be so choosy and must eat whatever nature will give them.

Understanding the Food Chain

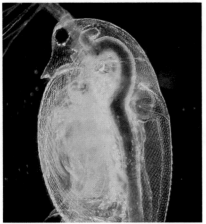

TINY ANIMALS, called *zooplankton,* feed on algae. This *daphnia,* or water flea, is stuffed with minute algae particles.

MINNOWS and other baitfish eat zooplankton. Some fish bypass this link in the food chain by feeding directly on algae.

SMALL GAMEFISH, such as sunfish and crappies, consume minnows and other small fish. However, they may feed directly on zooplankton.

How Foods Affect Fish Behavior

LARGE MASSES of food may suddenly appear, causing fish to switch diets. For example, walleyes stop eating perch during a mayfly hatch.

BAITFISH hatched in spring become large enough to interest predators by mid-summer. Fishing slows down when predators become glutted.

WINDBLOWN ALGAE can be a clue to fish location. Baitfish grazing on algae attract larger fish that find the murky water ideal for feeding.

PREDATORS eat whatever food is most available at the moment. Most predators prefer slim-bodied, soft-finned fish because they are easy to swallow. But when other foods are scarce, predators will consume deep-bodied, spiny-finned prey such as sunfish. For example, pickerel (above) and northern pike prefer perch, but often eat sunfish because they are abundant and live in the same type of habitat.

How Lures Attract Fish

MATCHING a lure to a known food is one way to make fish bite. Soft plastic worms and frogs look and feel like the real thing. Some manufacturers duplicate baitfish by applying photographs to lures.

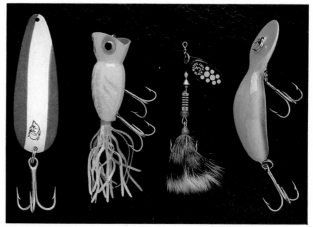

FLASH, vibration and color also attract fish. Spinners, red-and-white spoons, fluorescent plugs and yellow poppers look nothing like natural foods, yet they are among the most effective lures.

Cover

Fish discover the need for cover at an early age. From the day they hatch as *fry,* fish are constantly tested for their ability to survive. They must avoid larger fish, fish-eating birds, aquatic mammals, insects and other predators. Even with cover, nature takes a heavy toll. Some fish lay as many as 100,000 eggs. Less than one-third may hatch, and of these, only three or four fish may reach adulthood.

Adult fish also require cover to escape predators. Perch, for example, hide in weeds to avoid predators such as walleyes and northern pike. The weeds also help camouflage the perch, so they can dart out to grab minnows or other prey.

Some cover provides neither a place to hide nor a base for attack. Overhanging trees, for example, offer nothing but shade. Even so, they are an important source of cover for light-sensitive species such as largemouth bass.

Specific types of cover used by fish in lakes, reservoirs and ponds are shown on pages 30 to 33; cover common to rivers and streams on pages 40 to 43. Anglers who recognize different cover types can find gamefish faster.

Good Cover for Fish

DOCKS OR PIERS near thick weedbeds and drop-offs offer shade, food and easy access to deep water. Fish can easily move deeper without leaving cover.

BROAD-LEAVED weeds are preferred by most fish species, because they offer protection from predators and shelter from the sun's piercing rays.

Poor Cover for Fish

DOCKS OR PIERS far from deep water and dense weeds hold few fish. Most species are reluctant to cross an expanse of open water to reach these structures.

THIN-LEAVED weeds, unless extremely dense, give fish little security and almost no shade. Only small fish frequent weeds of this type.

Water

Fresh water differs in many ways. Color and clarity are two conditions which can be easily seen. Less obvious, though more important to fish, are temperature, oxygen level and fertility. Together, these factors determine the type and amount of fish in a lake and what part of the lake they inhabit.

TEMPERATURE. Each fish species requires a certain range of water temperatures in which to live, grow and reproduce. Fish fall into three categories according to temperature preferences. *Coldwater* fish are limited to lakes that provide a refuge of cold, oxygenated water in the heat of summer. *Coolwater* species fare best in waters with intermediate summer temperatures, but without long periods of high temperatures. *Warmwater* species thrive in lakes where temperatures are high all summer.

OXYGEN. The water in which fish live must have ample dissolved oxygen. Water absorbs oxygen when it comes in contact with the air. This is why

NASA INFRARED PHOTOGRAPH

WATER FERTILITY from three types of lakes is seen by the amount of algae in these samples. Though most kinds of fish inhabit more than one type of lake, the species indicated for each lake are most typical.

HIGH FERTILITY may be a problem in farmland lakes because nutrients wash in from surrounding fields. In summer, the deeper areas of the lake have no oxygen and no fish. Winterkill may occur.

flowing waters rarely have low oxygen levels. Oxygen is also added by aquatic plants. Fish extract oxygen as water passes through their gills. Crappies, northern pike, perch and especially bullheads tolerate lower oxygen levels than most gamefish.

FERTILITY. A lake's fertility is primarily determined by the amount of nitrogen and phosphorus in the water. These nutrients affect how many pounds of fish a lake can produce, just as the amount of fertilizer affects crop yields. Fertile waters have higher levels of these nutrients, so they develop heavy algae blooms. Since algae is the basic link in the food chain, these lakes produce many fish. Fertility also influences the type of fish a lake can support. Coldwater species such as trout cannot survive in fertile lakes. Bacteria decompose dead algae and plants on the bottom, consuming large amounts of oxygen and forcing fish into shallow water. There, coldwater fish would die from the high temperature.

In shallow, very fertile lakes, oxygen is used up rapidly in winter and thick ice and snow cover prevent aquatic plants from producing new oxygen. When conditions become too severe, even the most oxygen-tolerant species, such as bullheads, will die off. This is called *winterkill*.

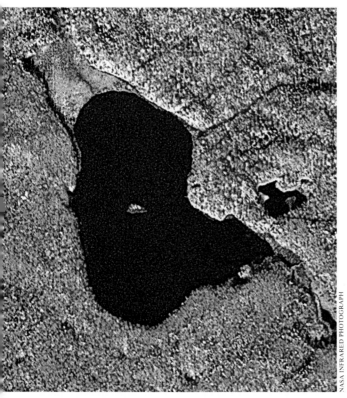

LOW FERTILITY limits the amount of fish in northern wilderness lakes. Surrounding lands are often rock, so rains wash in few nutrients. But the cold, oxygen-rich depths are ideal for coldwater fish like lake trout.

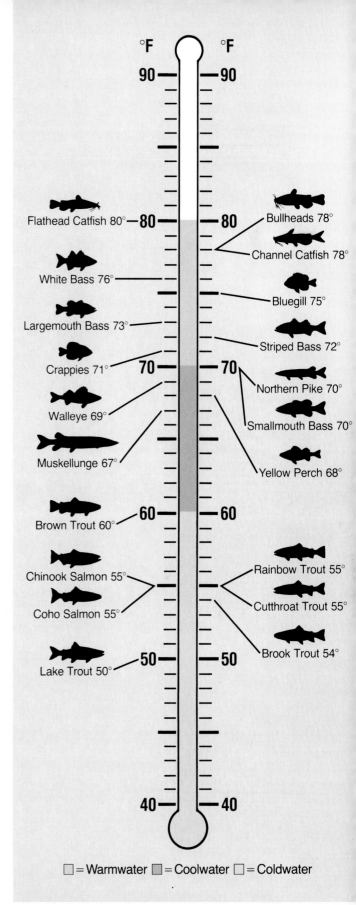

°F °F

Flathead Catfish 80° — 80 — 80 — Bullheads 78°
Channel Catfish 78°
White Bass 76°
Bluegill 75°
Largemouth Bass 73°
Striped Bass 72°
Crappies 71° — 70 — 70 — Northern Pike 70°
Walleye 69°
Smallmouth Bass 70°
Muskellunge 67°
Yellow Perch 68°
Brown Trout 60° — 60 — 60
Chinook Salmon 55° — Rainbow Trout 55°
Coho Salmon 55° — Cutthroat Trout 55°
Brook Trout 54°
Lake Trout 50° — 50 — 50

□ = Warmwater ▦ = Coolwater □ = Coldwater

TEMPERATURE PREFERENCES are different for most gamefish species. Although fish cannot always find the exact temperature they prefer, they are usually found in the water closest to that temperature.

The Fishes' World

Lakes

Every lake is unique, the end-product of a host of factors that combine to shape its character, including its fish population. Among these factors are geographic location, size and shape of the basin, and water fertility. Scientists separate lakes into three broad categories based on water fertility.

INFERTILE LAKES. The lands surrounding infertile or *oligotrophic* lakes release few nutrients into the water. Most oligotrophic lakes are located on the Canadian Shield, a vast, rock-bound area that covers eastern Canada and dips into the northern states from Minnesota to Maine. Some oligotrophic lakes occur at high elevations where the climate is cold. Coldwater species, such as trout, predominate. Because their fish are slow to grow and mature, these lakes can withstand little fishing pressure.

MODERATELY FERTILE LAKES. Classified as *mesotrophic*, lakes of intermediate fertility are located primarily in the northern United States and southern Canada. However, they can be found almost anywhere on the continent. Coolwater spe-

MOUNTAIN lakes, because of their altitude and rock-lined basins, are usually cold and produce few fish. This oligotrophic lake is home for cutthroat trout.

CANADIAN SHIELD lakes often have deep, rocky basins. Water in their depths is cold, though the shallows may be warm. Lake trout dominate in this oligotrophic lake.

SHALLOW, SHIELD lakes have warmer water, more vegetation and larger fish populations than deep Shield lakes. This mesotrophic lake contains walleyes and smallmouths.

cies dominate, though most support warmwater fish and a few have coldwater species.

FERTILE LAKES. *Eutrophic* or fertile lakes are surrounded by nutrient-rich soils which add large amounts of nitrogen, phosphorus and other fertilizing elements. They are typically found in agricultural areas in the southern two-thirds of the United States, although there are many in the North. Eutrophic lakes are best suited for warmwater fish.

Every lake is oligotrophic when first formed. As time passes, aquatic plants and animals die and their remains fall to the bottom to form a layer of organic ooze. As this layer thickens, the lake becomes shallower and is more easily warmed by the sun. Plant growth increases and the water becomes more fertile. At this stage, the lake is mesotrophic. Eventually, more ooze builds up on the bottom. The lake becomes shallower and warmer, so it reaches the eutrophic state. Finally, the water becomes too shallow for fish. This process, which may take thousands of years, is called *aging*. Below are six lakes which, from left to right, range from infertile to very fertile.

SHALLOW, SANDY lakes usually have warm water, moderate weed growth and a varied and abundant fish population. Walleyes, bass and panfish live in this mesotrophic lake.

CATTAIL-FRINGED lakes have muddy bottoms and heavy algae blooms. The depths usually lack oxygen. This eutrophic lake has largemouths, northern pike and bullheads.

MARSH lakes have plants growing throughout. In the North, they have few gamefish, but in the South, fish are plentiful. This eutrophic lake is noted for trophy largemouth bass.

21

Ponds

Natural and man-made ponds support about one-fourth of all freshwater fishing. Farm ponds alone total about 2½ million in the United States. They are created mainly to provide water for livestock or to control erosion. But hundreds of thousands have also been stocked with gamefish, providing new angling opportunities where fishable waters were once in short supply.

Ponds are popular with fishermen because they can usually be managed to yield more fish per acre of water than natural lakes. About 20 species of fish are stocked or occur incidentally in ponds. They vary from native brook trout that settle in a newly-formed beaver pond to channel catfish stocked and raised in a man-made pond.

The same factors that determine which types of fish inhabit a lake also decide which species can live in a pond. Most important are size, depth and location of the pond. However, water source has a greater impact on ponds than it does on lakes. For example, a spring flowing into a large lake has little effect on the lake's temperature. But a similar spring feeding a pond would chill the water enough to support trout. Unless springs are present or the basin is deep enough to stay cold in summer, a pond can support only warmwater or a few coolwater species.

FARM PONDS are usually man-made, formed by damming small streams or bulldozing shallow basins that fill with runoff. To support fish, ponds in the North should be at least 15 feet deep over half of the water area. Those in the South can be shallower. Largemouth bass and bluegills are the most popular farm pond species, although catfish are rapidly gaining popularity in the South. Some small, stagnant ponds harbor only bullheads.

BOG PONDS are typical of forested regions in the North. They are surrounded by spruce, cedar or tamarack trees. Sphagnum moss and other plants eventually form a spongy mat that covers much of the surface. Their waters are usually stained dark by acids from decaying vegetation. Northern pike, yellow perch and bullheads are typical species. In the aging process of lakes, bogs are the last stage that supports fish life.

MINE PITS or quarries often fill with ground water and runoff after mining operations cease. Ponds that are deep, infertile and cold are well-suited for trout. Some strip-mine pits have excellent largemouth fishing.

BEAVER PONDS can support such species as northern pike, largemouth bass, sunfish and crappies. Ponds linked to coldwater streams often hold trout. However, trout will move out if the pond gets too warm.

Reservoirs

Reservoirs are man-made lakes that form behind dams on rivers. They have characteristics of both lakes and streams. Like lakes, deeper reservoirs develop temperature layers and lose oxygen in their depths. Like rivers, some have current and hold typical river species such as catfish and white bass.

CANYON RESERVOIRS. Sometimes 500 feet or deeper, these steep-sided reservoirs have clear, infertile waters. Many have long, deep arms that are flooded valleys of feeder streams.

COVE RESERVOIRS. Most cove reservoirs are 50 to 200 feet deep. The arms are shorter and narrower than those of canyon reservoirs. Many arms are shallow and sprinkled with flooded timber. These reservoirs are moderately fertile and fairly clear, with a wide variety of fish habitat.

MARSHLAND RESERVOIRS. Called flowages in northern states, marshland reservoirs have extensive areas of flooded timber. Most are less than 50 feet deep and have large expanses of water 20 feet deep or less. Those in the South have fertile waters, ranging from fairly clear to turbid. Northern flowages usually have moderately fertile water.

CANYON RESERVOIRS support fewer fish than other man-made lakes because their fast-sloping bottoms produce little food. Most have bass and other warmwater fish, though some are better suited for trout.

STEEP ROCK WALLS are typical of canyon reservoirs. In dry years, water drawn off for irrigation may lower the water level 150 feet. As the water drops, fish change location, making angling difficult.

COVE RESERVOIRS have a variety of habitat and may support largemouth and smallmouth bass, crappies, walleyes, catfish, white bass and striped bass. Some deep cove reservoirs have trout.

NARROW ARMS often provide the best fishing in cove reservoirs. Flooded timber and brush in the upper ends of arms support bass and panfish. Lower, deeper portions of the arms may produce catfish and walleyes.

MARSHLAND RESERVOIRS in the South are havens for largemouth bass, including many over 10 pounds. Northern flowages usually have walleyes, muskies, northern pike and some bass and panfish.

FLOODED TIMBER is common in many marshland reservoirs. Although they seldom have well-defined arms or coves, they may have shallow bays with thick vegetation and flooded brush.

25

Fish Movement Through the Seasons

As the seasons pass, fish adjust to natural changes in lakes, reservoirs and ponds. Fish movement is keyed to two factors: dissolved oxygen and water temperature. Throughout the year, fish seek the zone in a lake that comes closest to satisfying *both* of these needs.

To understand how lakes change, it is important to know what happens to water at different temperatures. Water, like most substances, becomes lighter when warmed and heavier when cooled. But water has a unique property. When it cools below 39°F, it becomes lighter. This ensures that a lake's bottom water stays warmer than the surface during winter.

Because of this property of water, most lakes form three separate layers in summer. The upper layer, called the *epilimnion*, is warmer, lighter water that

Spring

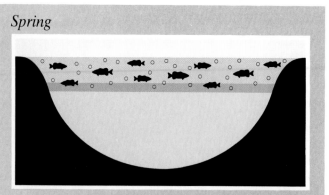

EARLY SPRING. The ice has melted. Runoff and the sun's rays rapidly warm a thin layer of water at the surface. As it warms, it absorbs oxygen from the air. Fish are drawn to the warm, oxygen-rich shallows.

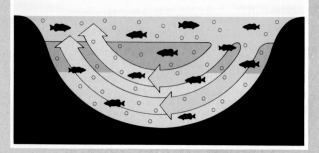

SPRING TURNOVER. When the surface water warms to 39°F, it sinks. Soon all water in the lake is 39°F, so density is the same from top to bottom. Wind easily mixes the water, spreading oxygen. Fish may be anywhere.

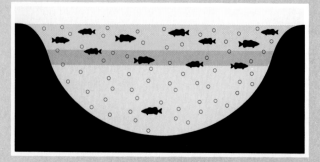

LATE SPRING. Warmer, lighter surface water starts to separate from cooler, heavier water below. Bottom water has oxygen, but is too cold for most fish. A strong wind can still mix the lake and scatter fish to any depth.

Summer

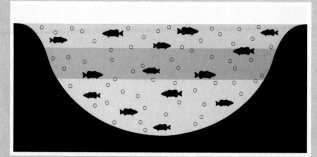

EARLY SUMMER. Three distinct layers form: the epilimnion or warm surface layer; the hypolimnion or cool bottom layer; and between them, the thermocline, where temperature drops fast. Fish select a comfortable depth.

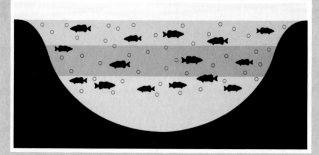

MID-SUMMER. Temperature layers become more distinct. The deepest part of the hypolimnion begins to lose oxygen. Coldwater fish are forced into the upper part of the hypolimnion, even though the water is too warm.

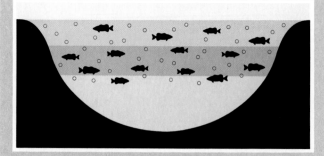

LATE SUMMER. Surface water has enough oxygen, but is too warm for many fish. The hypolimnion has lost much of its oxygen. Coldwater fish edge into the thermocline where warmer temperatures may kill them.

is easily circulated by the wind. As it mixes, it renews its oxygen supply. Meanwhile, the cooler, heavier bottom layer, or *hypolimnion,* becomes stagnant and may lose its oxygen. Separating the two layers is the *thermocline,* a zone where the temperature drops very fast. In very shallow lakes, however, these layers may not form because the entire body of water is mixed by the wind.

These diagrams show the annual cycle of a moderately fertile lake in a northern climate. Seasonal fish movement is different in other types of lakes. For example, infertile lakes do not lose oxygen in the depths, so fish are not forced into the shallows in summer or winter.

In extremely fertile lakes, low oxygen levels restrict fish to the shallows most of the year, with the exception of spring and fall turnover periods when they may be found anywhere.

○ = dissolved oxygen ▢ = warm water ▢ = cold water

Fall

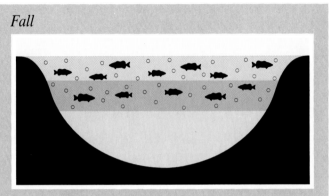

EARLY FALL. Cool nights lower the surface temperature. The margin between epilimnion and thermocline is less distinct. The hypolimnion remains unmixed and without oxygen. Many fish move to the cool shallows.

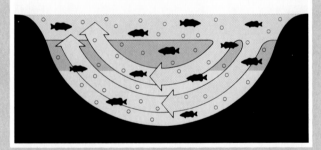

FALL TURNOVER. The surface water cools even more and begins to sink. The thermocline disappears. Soon, water at the surface is the same temperature as bottom water. Wind mixes the layers, scattering fish.

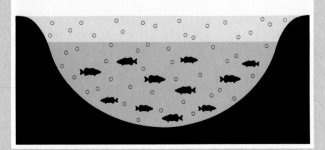

LATE FALL. The entire lake continues to cool, though faster at the surface. As the surface water drops below 39°F, it becomes lighter so it floats on the warmer, deeper water. Fish move to the warmer water.

Winter

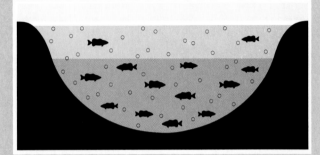

EARLY WINTER. Ice forms on a cold, still night, though the lake may re-open if milder days return. Fish may be found at any depth, but most stay in deep water where the temperature is warmer.

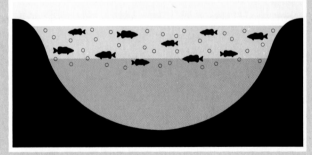

MID-WINTER. Thick ice and snow reduce the amount of sunlight reaching aquatic plants, so they cease to produce oxygen. Decaying plants and animals on the bottom consume oxygen, forcing fish to the oxygen-rich shallows.

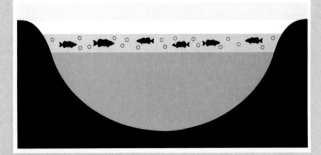

LATE WINTER. Ice and snow cover grows thicker. The low oxygen band widens. Soon, only the extreme upper layer has enough oxygen. A late winter thaw may bring oxygen into the lake. If not, it winter-kills.

Weather: How it Affects Fish

For centuries, the effect of weather on fish has been a source of controversy among fishermen. Izaak Walton, the father of angling, coined the phrase: "When the wind's from the east, fish bite least; when the wind's from the west, fish bite best." Some fishermen still believe Walton's words, though no scientific evidence has been found to prove his theory. Another point of argument is barometric pressure. Many anglers believe fishing is best when the barometer is rising. Others prefer to fish when pressure is falling rapidly. Here, too, science has failed to resolve the controversy.

Despite the disagreements, the following weather conditions definitely affect fishing success in one way or another for most gamefish species.

Conditions that Improve Fishing

WARM FRONTS usually bring fish into the shallows to feed. Wispy cirrus clouds and south winds generally signal the approach of a warm front.

MODERATE WINDS create a choppy surface, reducing light penetration. Light-sensitive fish like bass and walleyes move into the shallows to feed.

RAIN or cloudy conditions also cause light-sensitive fish to feed in shallow water. A light, warm rain is better for fishing than a heavy rainstorm.

Conditions that Cause Poor Fishing

COLD FRONTS send fish deep, making them sluggish. Black-bottomed clouds and northwest winds often signal a cold front's approach.

GLASSY WATER lets sunlight penetrate, causing light-sensitive fish to seek shade during midday. Light-tolerant fish such as bluegills still bite.

THUNDERSTORMS spook most gamefish, driving them to deeper water. Fishing usually remains poor for a day or two after a severe storm.

Structure: Where the Bottom Changes

When a fisherman looks at an unfamiliar body of water, he sees only a featureless surface. Choosing a fishing spot can be difficult, because almost every body of water has areas where the bottom drops off rapidly or where the type of bottom changes abruptly. These places usually hold more fish than featureless areas of the bottom. Fishermen refer to these areas as *structure*. Before fishing a lake, it is important to locate structure by examining a lake map (page 47) or sounding with a depth finder (page 52).

Anglers often confuse the terms structure and cover. Structure is a permanent feature on the lake bottom. Cover may vanish as weeds die off and logs decay. Fish use cover for shade or camouflage; structure may provide neither.

Common Types of Structure

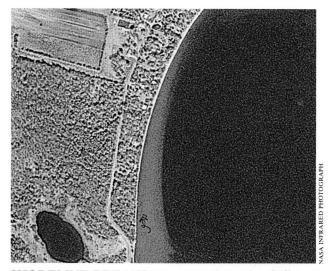

SAND BARS are found wherever a point of land juts into the water, or at the mouth of a stream. Fish feed on top of the bars in morning and evening, then drop off to the sides in midday.

SUNKEN ISLANDS, called reefs or humps, are simply hills jutting up from bottom. Those with firm tops and sides attract a variety of gamefish, especially in summer when many fish have moved away from shore.

SHORELINE BREAKS are areas where the shallows slope rapidly into the depths. A break is often marked by a weedline where water becomes too deep for rooted plants. Fish feed near the weeds and rest in deeper water.

ROCK OR GRAVEL patches attract fish, especially if the surrounding bottom is muck. Although these patches are the same depth as the adjacent bottom, they may be the only fish-holding areas in structureless lakes.

29

Cover: Where Fish Hide and Feed

Most gamefish spend a majority of their time in or near cover. For some fish, cover is a place to escape predators. But for the predators, it is a place of ambush. Some fish cannot tolerate bright sunlight, so they seek cover for shade. If cover is not available, they retreat to darkness in the depths.

Anglers should learn to recognize the wide variety of natural and man-made objects that provide cover for fish. A fallen tree is obvious cover. However, some cover is under water and must be found by using a depth finder, sounding with a fishing line, consulting lake maps or talking with fishermen.

On these pages are a few of the many cover types which attract fish.

LILY PADS attract bluegills and largemouth bass. Their wide, floating leaves provide shade, though the stems offer little cover. Fish use them regularly, but only if other cover is nearby.

HORSETAIL, BULRUSH and dense stands of other narrow-leaved plants are haunts for largemouth bass, bluegills and crappies. In spring, walleyes often frequent the fringes of bulrush beds.

FALLEN TREES are excellent cover for nearly every species of gamefish. Small branches harbor baitfish, while limbs and trunks provide shade and cover for larger fish, such as northern pike.

PONDWEEDS hide bluegills, bass, walleyes, pike and other fish. They usually grow in water less than 20 feet deep. Various types are found in the north-central and eastern United States and throughout Canada.

FLOODED TIMBER is a favorite hiding place for large-mouth bass in reservoirs. Best spots are along the margins of old stream channels where the trees end and the bottom drops off rapidly.

OVERHANGING TREES are sometimes the only source of shade for light-sensitive fish, such as large-mouth bass. Trees which shade drop-offs offer better fishing than those near extensive, shallow flats.

FLOODED BRUSH is found mainly in reservoirs where rising water has flooded streambank vegetation. Brush provides cover for largemouth bass, crappies and other shallow-water fish.

STEEP CLIFFS provide little protection from predators but they are excellent sources of shade. Fish use them most on bright days, but only when the sun is at the right angle to cast a shadow on the water.

SWIMMING PLATFORMS provide shade for bluegills, crappies and other panfish. Fish hover under them on sunny days. Platforms anchored over deep water attract more fish than those in the shallows.

ROCKS AND BOULDERS provide cover for catfish and other bottom-dwelling species in reservoirs, especially if there is current. Walleyes and smallmouth bass also prefer rocky bottoms.

SUNKEN LOGS attract many kinds of fish. They offer shade but provide little security. Log piles give more protection from predators because fish can hide in the spaces between logs.

BOAT DOCKS are a favorite source of cover for large-mouth bass, bluegills and crappies in lakes and reservoirs. Docks near drop-offs and thick weeds are usually best, especially for larger fish.

RIPRAP consists of rocks or concrete slabs dumped along a shoreline to prevent erosion. Large, loosely-spaced pieces make the best cover, especially if they are near deep water.

CLUTTER, including concrete blocks, tires and old car bodies, rests on the bottoms of most heavily-developed lakes. Although these objects are often difficult to find and to fish, they provide cover for many species.

FISH SHELTERS, constructed from logs or brush and weighted with rocks or concrete blocks, are placed in waters where natural cover is scarce. Insects and crusta-ceans living on the logs and branches attract baitfish.

Rivers & Streams

Beyond every bend in a stream lies a new fishing challenge, for no pool, riffle or rapids is just like the previous one. One moment the stream flows slowly over nearly level ground and the next, becomes a churning rapids as it plummets over steep terrain.

The slope or *gradient* of the streambed is one of many factors that determine which fish species live in a particular river or stream. Others include water chemistry, clarity, bottom type and depth. The overriding factor, however, is water temperature.

Spring-fed creeks, mountain streams and Arctic rivers never exceed 70°F. These coldwater streams usually host trout, steelhead, salmon, grayling or whitefish. Warmwater streams exceed 70°F for at least part of the year. They contain such species as largemouth and smallmouth bass, white bass, walleyes, catfish and carp.

To improve their fishing success, anglers should become more familiar with the various types of rivers and streams. Especially helpful is knowing how to *read* moving water and to recognize the haunts of river fish.

Below are four rivers and streams typical of flowing waters in North America.

SMALL TROUT STREAMS occur throughout much of the continent. Usually spring-fed, their waters are divided into recognizable pools, riffles and runs (page 38). This stream supports native brook trout.

LARGE TROUT STREAMS are common to mountainous areas of the West. Their current is fast and pools, riffles and runs are less distinct than in smaller streams. Rainbows, browns and cutthroats thrive in this stream.

SMALL WARMWATER STREAMS are most numerous in eastern and midwestern states and in southern Canada. Most have well-defined pools, riffles and runs. Smallmouth bass predominate in this stream.

LARGE WARMWATER RIVERS lace the eastern two-thirds of the United States. Many are dammed, so their waters appear as a series of long pools. Walleyes, largemouth bass, panfish and catfish live in this river.

Big Rivers

Large, warmwater rivers offer a wider choice of fishing opportunities than any other freshwater environment. A fisherman can catch a limit of scrappy white bass in the morning, battle a trophy northern pike at midday, cast for walleyes at dusk and that same evening, still-fish for flathead catfish.

Big rivers can support so many species of fish because their habitat is so diverse. Six or more distinct habitat types (below) may occur on rivers that have been dammed. A few fish species spend their lives in just one or two areas, though most move freely throughout the river system, especially when water levels change.

MAIN CHANNEL. Swift current and a bottom of fine sand or silt are typical main channel features. There is little vegetation or other cover for fish.

CHANNEL BORDERS. The channel border separates the main channel from shore. It may have man-made current deflectors or *wingdams* of rocks and sticks that force the current toward midstream to keep sediment from settling in the channel.

SIDE CHANNELS. Often called *cuts,* side channels connect the main channel with backwater lakes and sloughs. Their sand or silt bottoms are often choked with timber. The current is slow to moderate.

BACKWATER SLOUGHS. At normal water levels, backwater sloughs have no current. They have muck bottoms, dense growth of vegetation and very shallow water.

BACKWATER LAKES. Deeper than sloughs, backwater lakes have weeds only along their shorelines. Like sloughs, they have muck bottoms and little or no current.

TAILWATERS. Also called *tailraces,* tailwaters are stretches of turbulent water just below dams. They have rock, gravel or sand bottoms. Numerous *eddies,* places where current flows opposite of the main stream, are found along the channel margin.

MAIN CHANNEL waters seldom support large numbers of gamefish. Their current is too swift for most fish and they lack food and cover.

CHANNEL BORDERS often attract walleyes, white bass, smallmouths and catfish. Wingdams, downed trees and riprap shores draw the most fish.

SIDE CHANNELS are ideal for catfish. The current is slow and downed trees provide cover. Crappies and bluegills also hide among the limbs.

BACKWATER SLOUGHS hold northern pike, largemouth bass, bluegills and crappies. During high water, sloughs attract most river fish.

BACKWATER LAKES appeal to many species but are best for crappies and northern pike. Like sloughs, they draw fish when water is high.

TAILWATERS collect large numbers of fish in spring when dams block spawning migrations of walleyes, saugers and white bass.

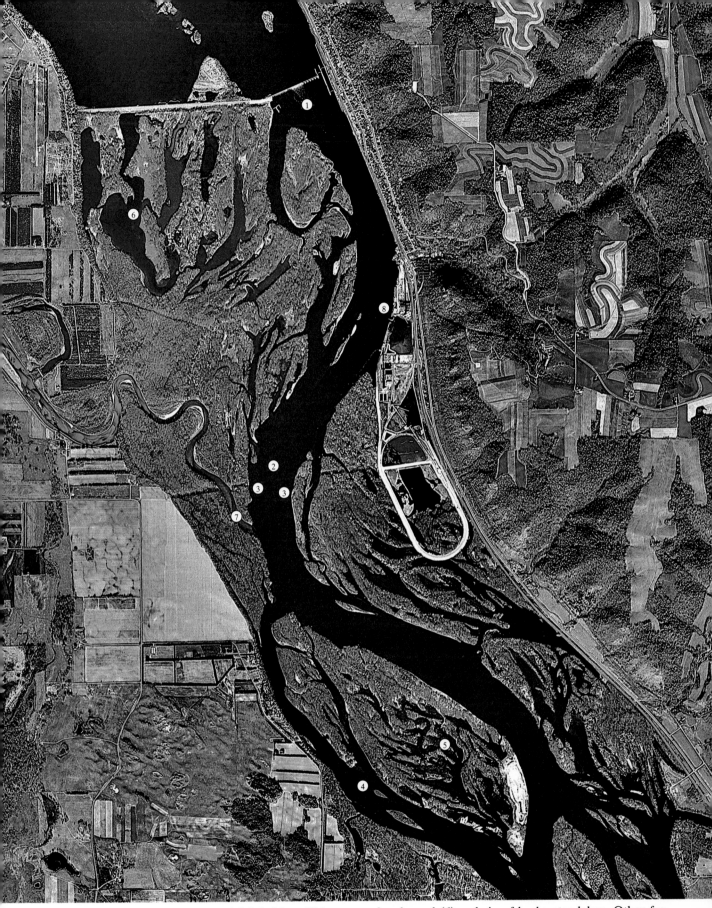

BIG RIVERS feature a vast array of fish habitat. This high-altitude, infrared photograph shows (1) tailwaters below a lock and dam, (2) main channel, (3) main channel border, (4) side channel, (5) a maze of backwater sloughs and (6) a chain of backwater lakes. Other features of interest include (7) a large tributary stream and (8) heated discharge water from a power plant, both potential fishing spots.

Small Rivers and Streams

Over one million miles of small rivers and streams crisscross the North American continent. Because many streams are lightly fished, they have excellent gamefish populations and offer anglers a chance to escape the crowd.

Most streams and small rivers have three distinct habitat types.

RIFFLES. Moderate to fast current and a turbulent surface are typical features of riffles. They have bottoms of gravel, rocks or boulders and are less than 2 feet deep. Extremely fast, whitewater riffles are called *rapids*.

RUNS. Runs are similar to riffles, but are deeper and less turbulent.

POOLS. Slow current and a surface that appears smooth on a calm day identify pools. They have bottoms of silt, sand or small gravel. Shallow pools are often called *flats*.

In slow-moving streams, pools are generally wide, while runs are narrow. In fast-flowing streams, riffles, runs and pools may be difficult to identify because they are nearly the same width. Nevertheless, fish recognize the different habitat types and so can the angler with a well-trained eye.

Species such as largemouth bass, crappies, catfish and walleyes spend most of their time in deep pools. Smallmouth bass and trout also inhabit pools but may be found in runs if the current is not too swift. Riffles are usually too shallow to provide enough cover for large fish, although they are important morning and evening feeding areas for many river species. Small gamefish and minnows stay in riffles throughout the day.

The photograph at right shows the typical riffle, run and pool sequence in a small stream. Numbers on the photo correspond to numbers on the diagram below which profiles the same section of stream.

RIFFLES, RUNS AND POOLS are formed by the awesome excavating force of moving water. Fast water in a riffle (1) digs a deeper channel or run (2). As the run deepens, the current slows, forming a pool (3). The slower current causes sediment to settle at the pool's tail or downstream end. As sediment builds up, the water

becomes shallower, channeling streamflow into a smaller area. Once again, the current speeds up, forming a new riffle. In most streams, this pattern is repeated about once for every seven stream widths. In other words, a new riffle, run and pool sequence would be repeated about every 140 feet in a stream 20 feet wide.

Where to Catch Fish in Rivers and Streams

Most river fish live along current margins or *breaks* where fast and slow water meet. They rest in calm water, then dart into fast water to grab food that floats by. This feeding behavior gives stream fishermen a big advantage. Because river fish do not have as much time to inspect a bait or lure, they are usually easier to catch than fish in lakes. The challenge is locating the areas that hold fish.

On most rivers and streams, patterns in the current reveal the location of eddies, wingdams, submerged rocks and other fish-holding areas. With a little practice, anglers can learn to identify these spots.

Experienced stream fishermen know that the best spots may change from day to day if water levels fluctuate. Eddies shift location as the water rises and the current gains speed. In large rivers, fish may abandon the main channel and move to adjacent backwaters with no current.

On the following pages are some of the common haunts of river fish. Some are easy to spot, while others require the ability to read moving water.

OUTSIDE BENDS in streams have the deepest water and strongest current. Soil along the riverbank is cut away by the current (arrows) and deposited along inside bends to create shallow sand or gravel bars.

UNDERCUT BANKS form along outside bends, wherever roots keep the surface soil from eroding. Trout and other fish often lie in the shade under a bank, where tree roots break the current.

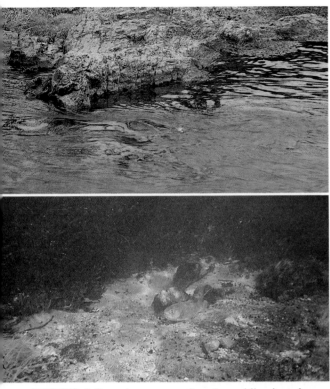

POINTS deflect the current, forming eddies just downstream. The swirling water scoops out deep pockets in the stream bottom. These pockets often hold more fish than any other spot on a river.

BRIDGE ABUTMENTS hold fish on both the upstream and downstream ends. Largemouth bass, walleyes, northern pike and catfish rest just below, while fast-water species such as smallmouth bass often lie just upstream.

FALLEN TREES and log jams deflect the current, causing it to erode deep holes around or under the branches. The trees provide both cover and current breaks for most kinds of river fish.

LARGE ROCKS break the river's current, creating areas of calm water that may extend several feet behind the rocks. To find rocks just beneath the water, look for Vs on the surface.

SHADE from overhanging trees often attracts species such as largemouth bass, walleyes and trout. When two areas are identical, the one with the most shade will hold more fish.

OVERHANGING GRASS along the streambank may be the best source of cover in trout streams that meander through meadows. Trout hide under the grass, snatching insects as they float by.

SPRINGS attract trout, northern pike or any species that seeks cooler water. However, springs in very cold trout streams have little impact because the temperature of the spring and stream are nearly the same.

ISLANDS usually create pockets of calm water at their downstream ends. Fish also lie in pockets and rocky areas along island edges, or near upstream ends where the current splits.

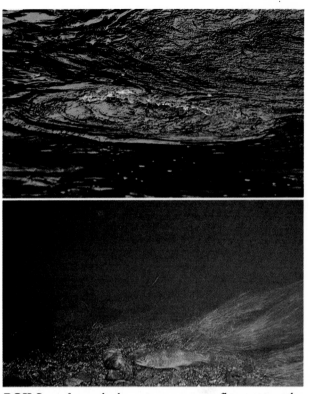

WINGDAMS are made of rock and saplings. They provide some of the best walleye, smallmouth and catfish habitat in big rivers. Fish usually lie just upstream, though some rest in the scour hole just below.

BOILS are formed when strong current flows over submerged boulders. Fishermen should not cast into a boil, but rather, several feet upstream. By doing this, the lure drops into the eddy just below the boulder.

BEAVER DAMS may improve or degrade trout habitat. On flat streams, dams back up too much water, making them too warm for trout. But on steep streams, pools above beaver dams may be the only spots that hold trout.

WARMWATER DISCHARGES attract most species of fish in cold weather. Catfish, white bass, largemouth and smallmouth bass, and other fish continue to feed in winter, even though the river water is near freezing.

Fishing Basics

Gathering Information

FREE INFORMATION is available from state and provincial fish and wildlife agencies. These materials help anglers find likely fishing areas and nearby access sites, and provide tips and regulations for catching fish.

A little homework prior to a fishing trip will pay big dividends later. When planning a trip, whether it be for lake trout in the Arctic or for bluegills in a pond near home, the fisherman would be wise to gather information that will make the outing more enjoyable and successful.

Natural resource and tourism agencies throughout North America provide valuable information for fishermen. They range from general publications that describe waters over a large geographical area to fish population surveys on certain lakes or streams. Whenever requesting information from government agencies, be as specific as possible.

Of all the materials available to anglers, maps are the most important. Highway maps will show the general location of lakes and streams, but more detailed county maps may be needed to find the access roads. Once there, the fisherman can save a great deal of time with a good lake map or river chart in hand. These materials are often free or available for a slight charge from various sources, including state fisheries and highway departments, U.S. Fish and Wildlife Service, U.S. Forest Service, Corps of Engineers, Tennessee Valley Authority, U.S. Geological Survey, power companies and other private sources.

Another time saver is hiring an experienced local guide. In just a few hours, a guide will reveal the top fishing spots, techniques, tackle and lures, saving the fisherman hours of experimenting and exploring. Considering the other expenses involved in a fishing trip, a guide's fee is a bargain.

Local anglers, resorters, bait-shop operators, game wardens, reservoir managers and water safety patrolmen can also provide vital information for fishermen. Other anglers are not likely to reveal their favorite spots, but they can often be pursuaded to point out well-known fishing areas and provide some tips on good baits and lures, best fishing times, and depths where fish are being caught. If a reliable source of information is found, write down the name and telephone number for future use.

LAKE MAPS, also known as hydrographic or contour maps, show many features of interest to fishermen including (1) steep drop-offs, indicated by closely-spaced contour lines; (2) gradually-sloping bottoms; (3) sunken islands, shown by a series of circles with the shallowest depth at center; (4) deep holes, with the greatest depth at center; (5) rocky reefs; (6) inlets; (7) boat ramps; (8) points or other landmarks; (9) boat liveries.

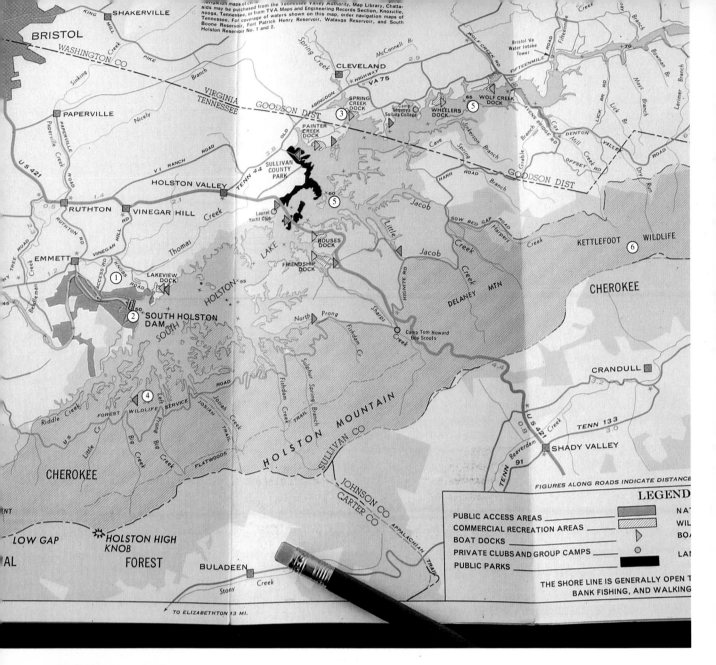

RESERVOIR MAPS identify (1) public access areas, (2) dams, (3) boat docks and recreation areas, (4) boat ramps, (5) location markers, which are important guides for anglers unfamiliar with a reservoir. Most maps also identify (6) state and federal wildlife management areas and game refuges. Others designate flooded timber and artificial brush piles.

A DEPTH FINDER, used with a lake or reservoir map, makes it easier to find fishing spots. Study the map to identify areas likely to hold fish, then use the depth finder to scout for specific structure.

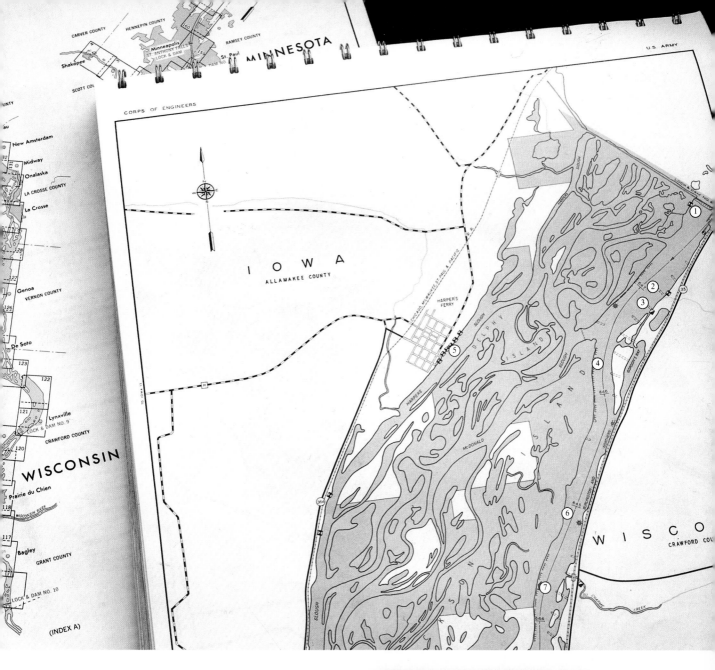

RIVER CHARTS are available from the Corps of Engineers either as single sheets or as a series of maps that trace segments of navigable rivers through several states. Most charts show (1) locks and dams, (2) submerged wingdams, (3) boat ramps, (4) riprap streambanks, (5) resorts, (6) lighted and (7) unlighted mileage markers. On this map, green areas are government-owned lands.

BAIT SHOP operators can provide valuable information. Most are anxious to recommend lakes or streams where anglers are catching fish, and to point out lures and baits that are currently the most successful.

Observing Nature's Signs

Experienced fishermen constantly watch for natural events happening around them. Nature provides many clues that can help unravel the mysteries of fish behavior.

The seasonal activities of fish correspond to the flowering of certain plants, bird migrations and other events. For example, white bass generally spawn when dogwood trees are blooming. However, this date may vary as much as three weeks from one year to the next.

The angler who times his fishing trip by the calendar has little chance of finding white bass on their spawning grounds year after year. But by waiting for the dogwoods to bloom, he can improve his odds of being there at the right time. With this in mind, many anglers keep logbooks of their observations to help them on future outings.

Other changes provide hints as to the whereabouts of fish. A sure sign of fall turnover in a lake (page 27) is a sudden decrease in water clarity. This tells the angler that fish are once again scattered top-to-bottom throughout the lake.

Sharp-eyed anglers are always alert for signs of fish activity. They keep a lookout for sunfish or crappies building their nests, for a big bass or pike feeding in the shallows or minnows dimpling the surface of a quiet bay. These and many other natural clues can prove invaluable to all fishermen.

INSECT HATCHES are sometimes so heavy that buildings and vegetation near the water are covered with insects. In western streams, the salmon fly hatch triggers a trout feeding spree.

SMALL FISH in the shallows during the day may mean that gamefish will move in to feed at dark. Some fishermen wear polaroid glasses so they can spot minnows in shallow water.

REDBUD TREES blossom when crappies spawn in many southeastern reservoirs. The flowering of many other trees and shrubs coincides with spring spawning runs of other gamefish such as bass and walleyes.

GULLS circling and diving over the water may be feeding on shad driven to the surface by white or striped bass. Anglers scout for this activity in late summer and fall, then move in to enjoy a fishing bonanza.

SPRING HOLES are easily found in winter. Carefully note their location, because they are often the key to finding fish, such as northern pike, during the hottest days of summer.

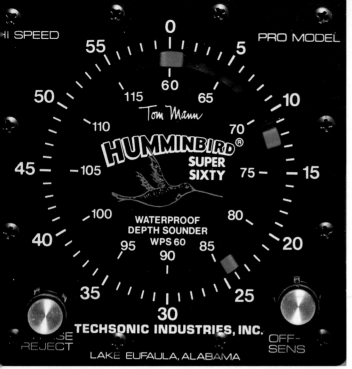

Electronic Aids

Electronic fishing aids have eliminated much of the mystery of finding gamefish, but certainly not the fun. Flashers, graph recorders, temperature gauges and other devices have made angling more enjoyable and successful for countless fishermen.

In years past, anglers had only a vague idea of water depth and shape of the lake bottom. Sonar equipment, however, has taken away much of the guesswork. Now, a fisherman simply has to learn how to read his equipment to determine the depth and to recognize structure, cover and fish.

FLASHERS or other sonar devices must be adjusted carefully. The *gain* or sensitivity knob should be turned high enough to produce a double echo. With the gain set too low, the unit will not detect fish.

HARD BOTTOM returns the strongest sonar signal. A second or third echo appears at low gain settings.

SOFT BOTTOM absorbs the signal so it shows up as a weak mark. The gain must be set high to yield a reading.

WEEDS appear as thin marks, but so can fish. If the signal moves when the boat is at rest, the marks are fish.

DROP-OFFS are indicated by wide marks, increasing in width as the slope of the bottom increases.

BOTTOM-HUGGING fish appear as distinct lines just above bottom. Signal width indicates size of the fish.

SUSPENDED fish, such as crappies, appear as tightly-spaced lines that come and go when the boat is still.

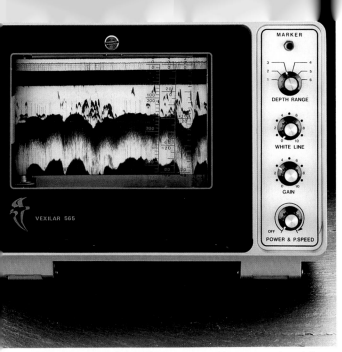

GRAPH RECORDERS convert the sonar signal into marks on paper. More powerful than flashers, they are capable of detecting fish as small as minnows. The depth of the mark indicates the relative size of the fish.

VIDEO SONAR units produce the same display as other graphs, but on a screen instead of paper. These units are popular with some fishermen because they do not require changing paper.

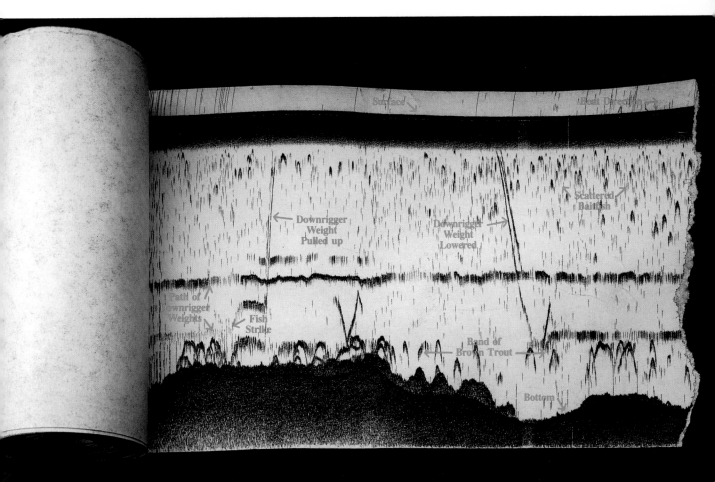

GRAPH TAPES provide anglers with permanent records of their fishing trips. By studying the tapes, they can learn more about the types of areas likely to hold fish.

This tape reveals a school of brown trout concentrated in a narrow band. By trolling a lure just above the fish, the angler was able to catch a large trout.

Fishing Boats

Fishermen select a boat with two things in mind. First, it must be safe for the waters they plan to fish. Second, it should be laid out and rigged for their style of fishing.

For example, a jon boat is ideal for fishing on shallow streams, but its low profile would make it too dangerous to use on large lakes. A bass boat is best for casting, but the transom is too low for back-trolling on a windy day. Console steering gives fishermen better forward vision for speeding from one spot to another, while tiller operated boats offer

SEMI-V boats are generally 12 to 16 feet long. They are inexpensive, yet versatile. Larger, deeper models are used on big lakes, while lighter models can be carried on car-top racks to waters without boat ramps.

BASS boats offer speed, comfort and efficiency. Fiberglass hulls are fast and luxurious, though the more economical aluminum hulls are becoming very popular. Some bass boats handle motors up to 150 horsepower.

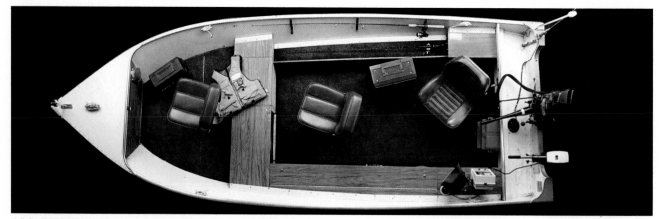

ALL-PURPOSE boats can be adapted for any of several angling techniques. Tiller steering makes back-trolling easier, while the flat, front deck aids casting. Most have semi-V hulls, live wells and large storage compartments.

better control and maneuverability. Many boats have comfortable swivel seats and flat, open floors so the angler can easily move around to cast or to fight a fish.

Modern boats are rigged with many sophisticated accessories. Sonar gear has become so popular that some boats are rigged with one or two flashers and a graph recorder. Electric trolling motors offer silent power and enable the fisherman to slow the boat to a crawl. Many boats have temperature gauges, bilge pumps, anchor winches, spotlights, compasses and CB or marine band radios.

Below are six boats that represent the major types used by today's fishermen.

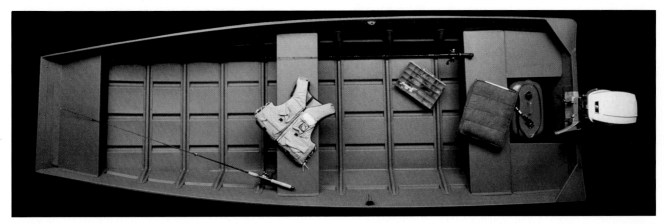

JON boats are rugged, inexpensive and stable. Their shallow draft makes them perfect for stumpy backwaters, marshy lakes and rock-strewn rivers. They can be paddled, poled or operated with a motor.

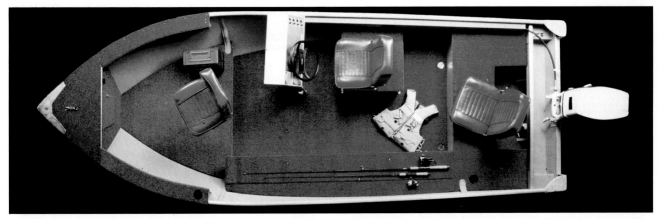

PIKE boats are popular throughout the northern United States. They combine the console steering and comfort of bass boats with the high-sided, semi-V hulls favored by fishermen on large lakes and reservoirs.

CANOES enable fishermen to reach small lakes, ponds and rivers where access is difficult. Square-stern canoes can accommodate small outboard motors. Standard models can be outfitted with a motor bracket.

Lines

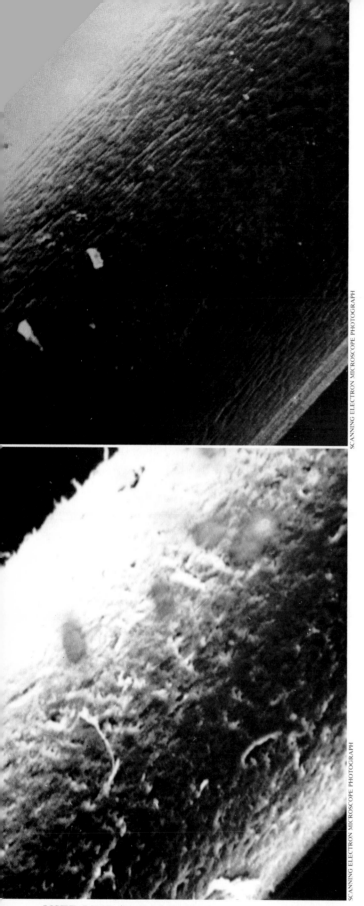

SCANNING ELECTRON MICROSCOPE PHOTOGRAPH

SCANNING ELECTRON MICROSCOPE PHOTOGRAPH

USED LINE (bottom) shows signs of wear compared to new 10-pound, nylon monofilament. Abrasion, chemicals in the air and many other factors deteriorate line. These lines are enlarged 400 times actual size.

The age of synthetics has given fishermen a wider selection of lines than ever before. Today, there is a line for virtually every angling situation.

MONOFILAMENT LINES. Used by spinning, spin-casting and many bait-casting fishermen, mono line is easy to cast, inexpensive, nearly invisible in water and very strong for its diameter. Monofilament differs greatly in quality. Premium mono is durable and its diameter is consistent. Cheap mono weakens quickly with use and often has thin spots.

Many types of monofilament line are available. Highly-visible or even fluorescent mono is favored by many plastic worm and jig fishermen who need to see the subtle line twitch that indicates a strike. Abrasion-resistant mono is preferred by those who fish in rocky lakes or streams. Thin, flexible monofilament is used by live-bait fishermen who want to present the bait naturally.

BRAIDED LINES. Whether nylon or dacron, braided lines stretch very little, so they are good for sinking a hook into hard-mouthed fish such as northern pike. Braided lines are commonly used on bait-casting reels.

FLY LINES. Fly fishermen choose from four basic lines. *Level,* though not widely used, is the same diameter over its entire length. It is an all-purpose line. *Double taper* line has a level middle section or belly, but gradually tapers at each end. It presents flies delicately and is economical to use. When one end wears out, simply reverse it and use the other end. *Weight forward* line has a short, thick belly just behind the tapered front end. The back portion is level line. The extra weight up front enables the fisherman to make longer casts or punch into a strong wind. *Shooting head* is similar to weight forward line, except the back portion is monofilament. It can be cast farther than any other line. Most fly lines are designed to float, but sinking or sinking-tip models are available. All shooting head lines are made to sink.

Numbers designate the weight of fly lines. No. 2 is the lightest and No. 11 the heaviest. For best casting performance, the line must be matched to the rod.

SPECIAL PURPOSE LINES. Monel wire lines are designed for extremely deep trolling. Lead-core lines are more flexible and easier to work with, but do not sink quite as deep. Some speed trollers use color-coded mono lines that help determine how deep their lures are running.

Knots

A fishing line is only as strong as the knots in it. All knots weaken line. The best have little effect on line strength, while the worst cut strength in half.

The knots on pages 58 and 59 work well for the purposes described, though many other knots can be used. Two favorites, the clinch and improved clinch are not recommended, because few fishermen tie them consistently well. As a result, these knots often have sharp bends which fracture under stress. Choose knots that are easy to tie correctly, because even the strongest knot is weak if not properly tied.

Knots weaken with use. Good fishermen tie new knots before a trip and test their knots frequently.

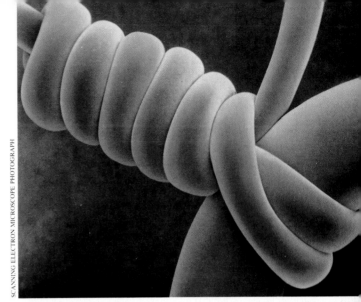

THE TRILENE KNOT is unusually strong. It is rated at 90 percent of the line strength, compared to an average strength of about 75 percent for other fishing knots. This knot was tied with 10-pound mono and enlarged 40 times.

TIE knots carefully. A slight scratch from a clippers is barely visible to the human eye. But reproduced 40 times actual size, the nick in this improved clinch knot appears as a large rupture in the line's skin.

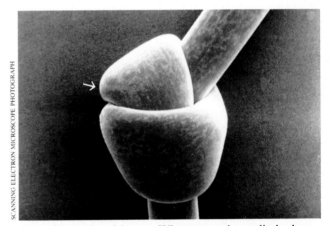

AVOID overhand knots. When stress is applied, sharp edges (arrow) cause the skin to fracture, greatly reducing its strength. Shown is an overhand or wind knot in 10-pound mono at 50 times actual size.

Tips for Tying Knots

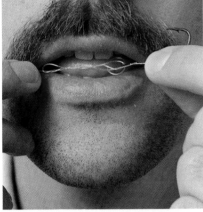

MOISTEN the knot with saliva before snugging it up. This reduces friction and helps to form a knot that is smooth and tight.

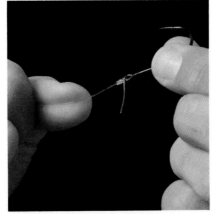

SNUG up the knot with a smooth, strong pull. Do not be timid about testing it. Better that it breaks while being tied, than after hooking a big fish.

CLIP the tag end of the line carefully. It pays to leave a little extra line, because all knots slip slightly just before they break.

Basic Knots Every Fisherman Should Know

Knowing how to tie these six knots will prepare the fisherman for virtually every angling situation. For demonstration purposes, these knots were tied with extra-heavy line.

Hook to Line: Trilene Knot, Strength 90%

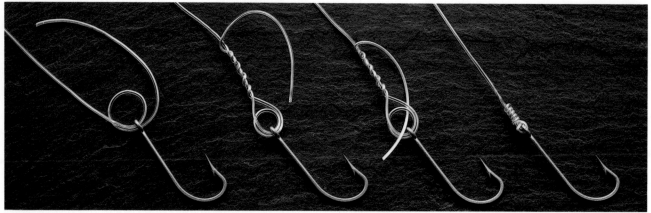

PASS the line through the eye of the hook twice from the same side. Leave a small loop next to the eye. Wrap the free end of the line around the standing line five times. Then, insert the free end through the double loop next to the eye. Snug up with a firm steady pull on the line and the hook.

Hook to Line: Palomar Knot, Strength 85%

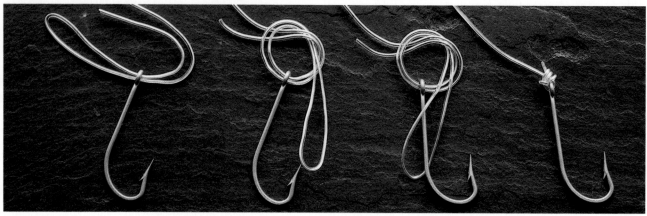

FOLD the line against itself to form a double strand. Next push the end through the eye of the hook. Tie an overhand knot in the double strand, leaving a loop big enough to pass the hook through. Snug up the knot by pulling on the hook with one hand and the double strand with the other.

To Form a Loop: Double Surgeon's Loop, Strength 70%

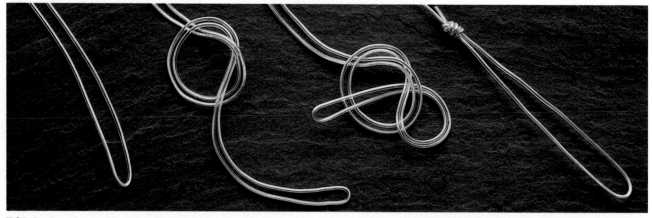

FOLD the line against itself to form a double strand. Next, tie an overhand knot in the double strand. Pass the end of the double strand through the opening in the overhand knot again, then tighten firmly. Loops are often tied at the end of a leader, so they can be attached quickly to a snap or to another loop.

Line to Spool: Improved Arbor Knot, Strength 60%

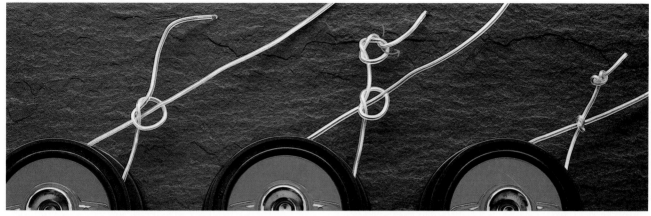

LOOP the line around the spool, then tie an overhand knot around the standing line to form a loose slip knot. Tie an overhand knot in the free end. Next, pass the free

end through the overhand knot again (arrow). Snug up the knot in the free end, then pull firmly on the standing line to tighten the knot around the spool.

Lure to Loop: King Sling, Strength 75%

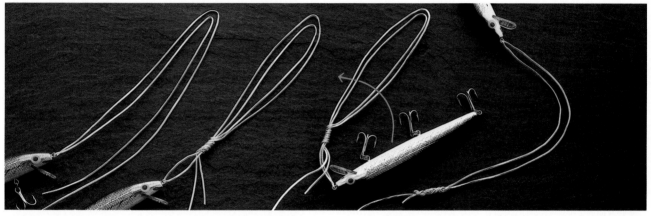

PASS the line through the eye of the lure to form a double strand. Form a large loop in the double strand and twist it three times. Drop the lure through the loop (arrow) and

snug up the knot with a steady pull. The loop allows the lure to swing freely as it is pulled through the water, providing the best possible action.

Line to Line: Blood Knot, Strength 65%

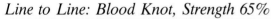

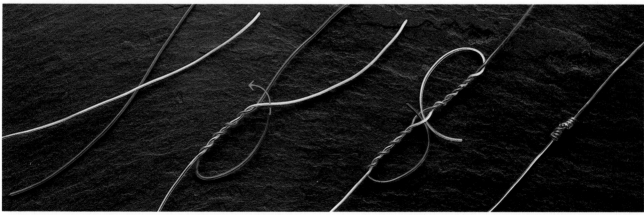

OVERLAP the lines so they point in opposite directions. Twist one line four times around the other, then bring the free end back and insert it between the two lines (arrow).

Twist the other line the same way and bring it back through the same opening that holds the other line. Tighten the knot with a jerk.

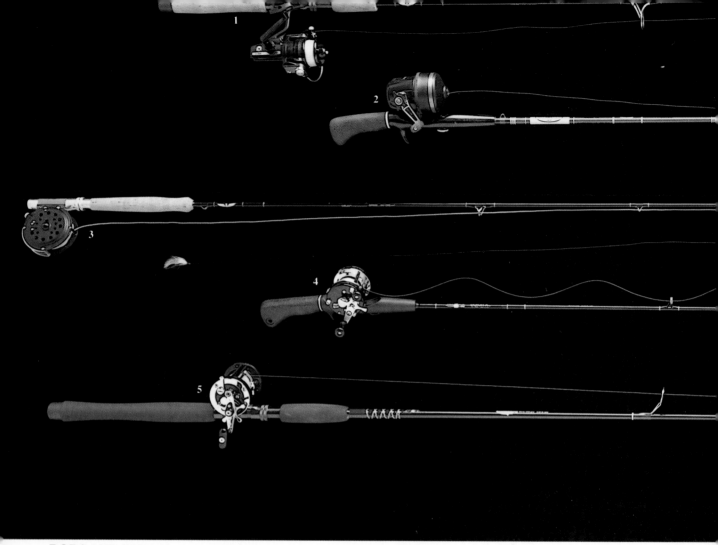

RODS AND REELS include: (1) Spinning rod with open-face reel, (2) spin-cast rod with closed-face reel, (3) fly rod with

Rods & Reels

Many fishermen use only one rod and reel for a variety of angling purposes. Certainly, a 6- to 6½-foot, medium-action spinning outfit is acceptable when bobber-fishing for crappies, casting spoons for northern pike or trolling for walleyes. Some situations, however, demand a specific rod and reel combination. For example, casting a tiny, weightless fly requires fly-fishing tackle. Or, casting a foot-long muskie plug is possible only with a stout rod and heavy-duty reel.

Anglers who regularly switch from one type of fishing to another carry as many as four rods, each rigged and ready for different kinds of fish. Not every fisherman needs that much tackle, but at least one backup rig is a good idea.

Following are five basic rod and reel combinations:

SPINNING. Spinning tackle is popular because it is versatile, backlash-free, and designed for extra casting distance. The open-face reel allows line to whip off a fixed spool. The rod has large guides, so

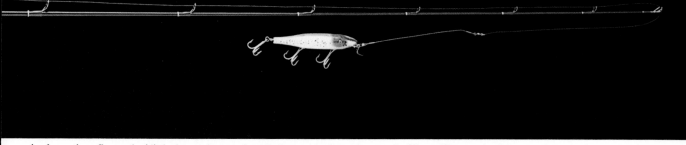

single-action fly reel, (4) bait-casting rod with free-spool casting reel, (5) trolling rod with star-drag reel.

coils of line can flow through with little friction. One drawback to the open-face reel is that beginning anglers may have trouble with line snarling behind the spool.

SPIN-CASTING. Spin-casting equipment offers many of the same advantages of spinning tackle. The closed-face design of the reel reduces tangling and its push button line release makes casting easier. However, the reel's closed face increases line friction, which reduces casting distance. Spin-casting reels clamp to the top of the rod handle, while spinning reels attach underneath the rod.

FLY-CASTING. Fly reels are not as important as other types of reels. Their primary function is to store line. Fly rods are usually quite long. The shorter rods are 7½ feet, while many exceed 9 feet in length. Most fly rods are designed to flex from tip to butt. This whipping action helps the angler pick up and cast long lengths of line.

BAIT-CASTING. Bait-casting tackle excels for casting accuracy. Modern reel design has all but eliminated backlashes, once a constant headache for many fishermen. Bait-casting rods, especially those used to cast heavy lures or crankbaits, are stiffer than spinning rods.

TROLLING. Rods and reels used for big-water trolling are similar to bait-casting outfits, but are much heavier. Trolling reels are rugged, store a lot of line and have smooth drags. Because they are not designed for casting, they are less expensive than fine-tuned bait-casting reels. Trolling reels do not have the line-twist problems of spinning reels.

Choosing the Right Rod for the Job

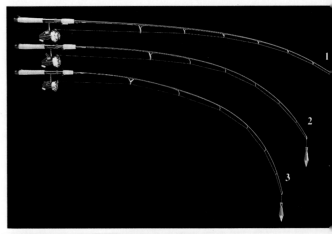

ACTION is demonstrated by lifting equal weights with different rods. A fast-action rod (1) bends near the tip. A medium-action rod (2) starts to bend near the middle. A slow-action rod (3) bends over its entire length.

Fishermen must choose from a wide array of rods, many designed for specific purposes. Before making a selection, it is important for anglers to understand basic rod qualities.

Action refers to where a rod bends. It is determined by the degree of taper in the rod shaft. *Power* or strength is the amount of force needed to bend the rod. It is determined by the thickness of the shaft walls. Many fishermen, and even some rod manufacturers, confuse the terms action and power. When buying a rod, remember that when a salesman talks about light-, medium- or heavy-action rods, he is referring to power instead of action.

Sensitivity is the ability of the rod to telegraph vibrations from the line through the tip and on to the hand. It is determined by the material and by the rod's action. A fast-action rod is generally more sensitive than a slow-action rod of the same material.

Rod materials differ in many ways. Fiberglass is durable, economical and well-suited to most angling situations. Graphite is stronger and more sensitive, but is more expensive than fiberglass. Boron is slightly stronger and more sensitive than graphite, but is even more expensive. Bamboo requires more care and lacks the power of space-age materials. It is mainly used for custom-made fly rods.

Length, by itself, should not be a major consideration when choosing a rod. However, length is important in certain situations. A short rod works best for casting in tight quarters, while a long rod is essential for long-distance casting. The current trend is toward shorter, thinner rods that are equally as powerful as the longer, thicker rods of years past.

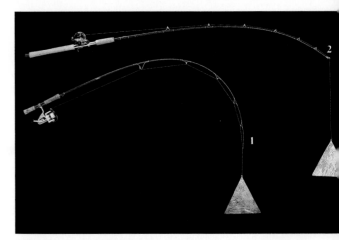

POWER or strength is shown by lifting 2-pound weights with (1) an ultralight spinning rod and (2) a heavy-duty casting rod. The spinning rod doubles over from the weight, while the casting rod flexes much less.

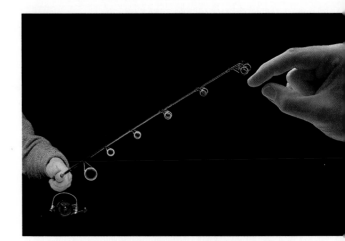

SENSITIVITY can be tested by gently tapping the rod tip with a finger. With a sensitive rod, the vibrations are easily felt at the handle. A sensitive rod makes it easier to feel bottom and to detect bites.

FAST-ACTION rods are good for working a surface popper, jigging, setting the hook or other uses which require a responsive tip.

SLOW-ACTION rods are often used with downriggers. As a fish strikes and the line releases, the rod pops out of its deep bend, taking up slack line.

FIGHTING FISH is easier with a slow rod. The added flex acts like a shock absorber, keeping the line tight while the fish thrashes.

ULTRALIGHT rods bend with only a light weight, making it possible to cast tiny lures. They make small fish feel big to the angler.

HEAVY-DUTY rods are needed to cast big lures such as muskie plugs. They also have the power to drive the hooks into a muskie's bony jaw.

OBSTACLES such as timber and thick weedbeds make it necessary to use a rod with enough power to stop a fish's run and keep it away from snags.

MATERIALS shown have equal power. Boron (right) is thinnest and most sensitive, followed by graphite (center) and fiberglass (left).

FERRULES, especially metal ones (top), reduce sensitivity. Fiberglass or graphite ferrules are better; one-piece rods are best of all.

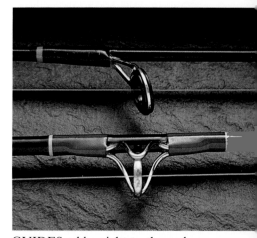

GUIDES add weight to the rod, reducing sensitivity. Single-foot guides (top) are light and retain sensitivity better than conventional guides.

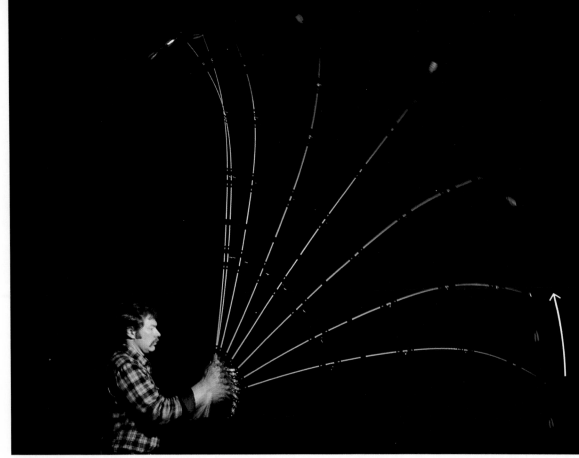

THE BACK CAST starts (arrow) with a fast upward motion of the forearm and wrist. Stop the rod when it is nearly vertical. The weight of the lure will bend or *load* the rod, as shown in this multiple-exposure photograph.

Casting

Casting is the best angling technique when fish are holding tight to cover, concentrated in dense schools or hiding in areas where they would be easily spooked if the fisherman moved too close.

Accurate casting is necessary in many situations. A bass lying under a log often ignores a lure unless it is placed within inches of its mouth. A fly fisherman casting to a rising trout must hit a target less than one foot in diameter.

For maximum casting accuracy, use a medium-action rod. A rod that is too stiff results in the angler throwing the lure rather than casting it. A rod that is too whippy makes it difficult to control the direction of the cast.

Casting distance is important when approaching spooky fish or when trying to reach open-water fish from shore. For maximum distance, use a long, powerful rod with guides that are spaced close enough together so the line flows freely. On spinning or spin-cast reels, fill the spool to within one-eighth inch of the rim to avoid friction when the line whips off the spool.

ACCURACY is easily attained by using a bait-casting reel. Keep the handle up, then cast the lure with a straight overhand motion. Thumb the reel to stop the lure at exactly the right spot.

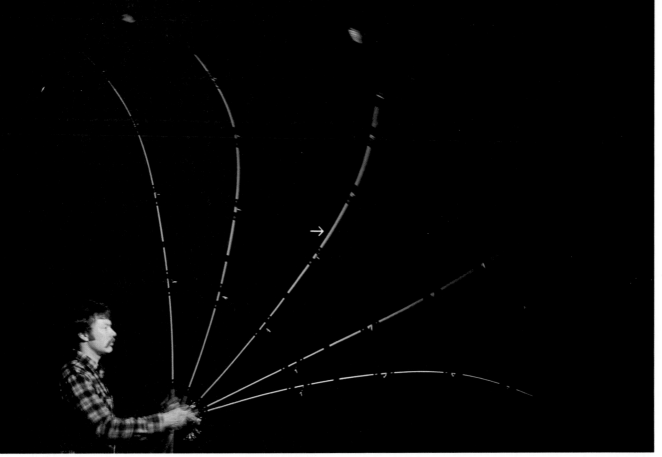

THE FORWARD CAST follows without delay. Again, using mostly wrist power, snap the rod forward in a quick downstroke. Release the line midway through the cast (arrow), so the lure travels in a straight line.

DISTANCE CASTING is often done with a two-handed grip on the rod. Snap the rod back sharply, loading it to its full potential. Then, whip it forward, releasing the line so the lure travels in a higher-than-normal arc.

FLY-CASTING involves throwing a line rather than a heavy lure. First, strip several yards of line from the reel. Start the back cast by slowly lifting the rod tip, rapidly increasing the tempo until the rod is vertical. Wait for a tug on the rod, a signal that the line has straightened out behind. Then, bring the rod forward with a smooth, powerful motion. For greater distance, continue the forward-backward motion while stripping out more line.

Trolling & Drifting

Trolling lures or baits aimlessly behind a boat, without regard for speed or water depth, is a waste of time. For best results, use a depth finder and carefully follow bottom contours. When a fish is caught, pinpoint the spot by tossing out a marker buoy. Then, troll back over the spot several times. Boat speed is important because some lures run better fast, others slow. Live bait is usually trolled very slowly.

Smart trollers carefully note the depth on their sonar units whenever they feel a strike or hook a fish. They continue to troll at the same depth, because water temperature and light penetration are likely to concentrate other fish at that level.

Controlling a boat is difficult on windy days. One solution is to troll into the wind, then let the boat drift back. Typical drifting speed is just about right for trailing live bait, but is too slow for most lures. Many anglers cast and retrieve lures as the boat drifts. A good tactic is to cast with the wind for extra distance; this way, the lure or bait covers water that has not been crossed by the boat. When drifting with live bait, fish on the side facing into the wind, so the boat does not drift over the lines.

FORWARD TROLLING works best with artificial lures. Try different colors and actions to find the lures that are most productive.

BACK-TROLLING allows precision boat control at slow speeds. Point the transom into the wind and operate the motor in reverse.

DRIFTING is a good technique when fish might be spooked by an outboard motor. Use oars or an electric trolling motor to adjust the boat's path.

Tips for Successful Trolling

TEST a lure by pulling it alongside the boat. Vary the trolling speed to find the best action. A lure trolled too slow has little or no action. A lure pulled too fast often tips on its side and runs to the surface.

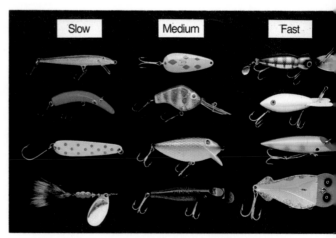

COMPATIBLE lures must be used when trolling with several lines. Above, are lures designed for slow, medium and fast trolling. If a slow-action lure is used with a fast-action lure, one is sure to run improperly.

TROLLING enables fishermen to cover large expanses of water quickly. It is especially popular on many large lakes, rivers and reservoirs, because it improves the angler's chances of locating individual fish scattered along miles of shoreline, or schools of fish in open water. Once fish are found, many anglers stop trolling and switch to a more thorough method such as jigging, slip-bobber fishing or casting with live bait.

TROLLING MOTORS powered by batteries move a boat silently and with excellent control. They are economical and produce no gas fumes.

DEPTH FINDERS help trollers follow drop-offs, making it easier to keep baits and lures close to the bottom or at a constant depth.

TROLL the lure above fish for best results. Because of the position of their eyes, gamefish can see above better than below.

JIGGING LURES include vibrating blades such as (1) Sonar; leadhead jigs such as (2) bucktail, (3) feather jig, (4) Mister Twister; tailspins such as (5) Zinger Shad; jigging spoons such as (6) CC spoon.

Jigging

Jigging is one of the most difficult techniques to master. But, it is a skill worth learning, because few fish can resist a jig's enticing action.

Retrieve a jig by twitching the rod tip, then allowing the jig to settle back to bottom. Fish usually strike as the jig is falling. Anglers frequently make a crucial mistake by letting the line go slack when the jig falls, making it impossible to detect a strike. A good fisherman uses a sensitive rod and always keeps the line tight. Even then, a strike feels only like a light tap.

Lures used for jigging include leadhead jigs, jigging spoons, vibrating metal blades and tailspins. These lures can be jigged vertically while slowly drifting or trolling. Or, they can be cast, allowed to sink and bounced along the bottom. Leadhead jigs are often tipped with minnows or some other type of bait.

Choose a jig that is heavy enough to reach bottom, but not too large for the target species. Experiment to find the right color and material. Many fishermen prefer soft-plastic bodies, because fish mouth them for an instant longer than other jigs, providing extra time to set the hook.

How to Jig-fish

CAST the jig and let it sink as demonstrated in this multiple exposure. Keep the bail open until the line hits bottom and goes slack.

HOP the jig, as shown in this multiple exposure. Keep the line tight as the lure falls back. Be alert for a tap while the jig is dropping.

SET the hook immediately after feeling a tap. Even the slightest delay gives the fish time to recognize the jig as a fake and reject it.

Still-fishing

Still-fishing is the most common method of angling, because it is easy, requires only basic equipment and when done properly, is extremely effective. The usual strategy is to cast the bait into a likely spot, then sit back and wait. Most anglers use live baits or other types of bait that attract fish by smell. Although still-fishermen must rely on the fish coming to them, they can do several things to improve their chances.

First, use fresh bait. Many anglers refuse to change bait, often for hours at a time. A lively minnow has much more appeal to a fish than a dead minnow hanging limp on a hook.

Second, fish near cover, structure or wherever fish are likely to concentrate. The angler who finds a comfortable spot and throws the bait out anywhere, has little chance of catching fish consistently.

Third, keep trying different spots and baits to find a combination that works. It rarely pays to fish the same spot for hours on end when nothing is biting. Many anglers troll or drift to locate fish, then switch to still-fishing.

DUSK AND DAWN are generally the best times to still-fish, because changing light levels trigger most fish to move about in search of food. However, species such as bluegills and pike usually bite better at midday.

Basic Still-fishing Rigs

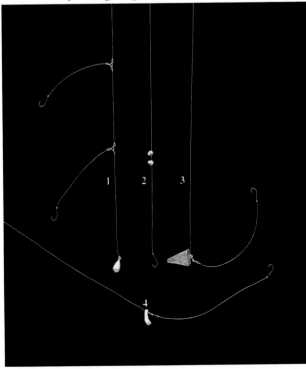

BOTTOM RIGS include (1) multiple-hook rig, for stacking baits at different depths; (2) split-shot rig; (3) pyramid sinker setup, to prevent the bait from drifting in strong current; (4) slip-sinker rig, for light biting fish.

BOBBER RIGS include (1) clip-type bobber, which slides easily on the line; (2) slip-bobber, for deeper water; (3) pencil bobber, which is the most sensitive; (4) lighted bobber, for night fishing.

Detecting the Strike

When a big salmon slams into a fast-moving lure, there is no doubt in the fisherman's mind as to what has happened in the depths below. But feeling bites is not always so easy, especially when using live bait.

When the fisherman suddenly feels an extra drag on the line, it could be a fish slowly swimming with the bait in its mouth or it might be a weed or stick. The best way to tell is to gently pull back on the rod tip. A fish will shake its head when it feels its food trying to escape. Only experience will tell how much an angler can pull before the fish drops the bait.

The most important thing a fisherman can do to fine-tune his sense of feel is to use a sensitive rod (page 62), one that readily transmits the vibrations from a biting fish.

SLASHING strikes are easy to detect. For example, when a largemouth bass or muskie sees a lure whiz by, it gives chase with a burst of speed and hits so hard that it often hooks itself.

How Different Fish Strike

INHALING the bait, as shown in this multiple exposure, is typical of bluegills and bass. They suck in the bait along with a quantity of water.

GRABBING is one way that predators, such as pike, strike small fish. They catch a minnow crosswise, run, then stop to swallow it headfirst.

NIBBLING is typical of small fish such as perch. They are difficult to catch, because they nip at loose ends of the worm and avoid the hook.

Tips to Help Detect the Strike

A SHORT LINE makes it easier to feel a bite. Excess line dragging on bottom soaks up much of the impulse that indicates a strike.

POLARIZED GLASSES reduce glare. A line twitch from a bite would be more easily seen in the photo at right, taken through polarized glass.

WEEDS are often mistaken for a bite. The hook tears through one leaf and snags another. The jerky pull feels much like a fish.

Setting the Hook

Even the best anglers lose fish by failing to set the hook properly, especially when fishing with live bait. Many beginning fishermen fear that if they set the hook too hard, it will rip out of the fish's mouth. This rarely happens. By the time the rod bends and the line stretches, only 1 or 2 pounds of pull is likely to reach the fish. Some expert anglers strain the rod nearly to the breaking point to make sure the hooks penetrate.

Always reel up slack line before setting the hook. After taking the bait, a fish may move off in any direction or double back leaving a large loop in the line. Setting the hook with too much slack line will only startle the fish, causing it to drop the bait.

Another mistake is using a rod that is too whippy. A rod that bends too easily lacks power to sink the hook. A loose drag can also be a problem. If the drag slips while setting the hook, much of the power is lost. Keep the drag fairly tight when fishing, then loosen it slightly while playing a fish.

SET the hook with a powerful upward sweep of the rod. Use as much force as the rod and line will bear. Some fishermen set the hook two or three times to be sure the barbs sink in.

How to Set the Hook When Bait-fishing

FEED line so the fish does not feel resistance while it runs. Walleyes, bass, northern pike and other fish often swim off in a crooked path, creating an *S*- or *U*-shaped bend in the line.

POINT the rod in the direction of the fish and quickly reel up slack line. Continue winding until the line tightens and the weight of the fish becomes obvious. Then, set the hook immediately.

71

Playing & Landing Fish

Every fisherman has heard stories about big ones that got away. Indeed, many trophy fish are lost, either because the drag was set improperly or the landing net was mishandled.

When playing a fish, keep the rod tip high so the rod and your arms can absorb some of the stress when a fish runs. If the reel has an anti-reverse mechanism, make sure it is off. Then, if the drag malfunctions and the line nears the breaking point, simply turn the reel handle backwards to relieve tension. Some fishermen refuse to rely on a drag. Instead, they tighten the drag and fight the fish by back-reeling.

As the fish nears the boat, the angler should guard against spooking it into a last-ditch run that might snap the line. Common mistakes are trying to land a fish before it is tired, keeping the net in the water and attempting to net a fish tail-first.

A TIGHT LINE is essential when fighting a fish. If the line goes slack, the fish may throw the hook, especially if it is not set firmly. Keeping a taut line is difficult when the fish leaps or thrashes on the surface. As a result, species which tend to jump, such as bass, trout and muskellunge, escape more often than gamefish that fight deep.

DRAGS, shown on spinning (top), spin-casting (middle) and bait-casting reels (bottom), must be properly set. If too loose, the drag will slip when setting the hook. If set too tight, a big fish will snap the line.

SET the drag only after line has been threaded through the guides. Pull the line with one hand, while holding the rod firmly with the other. Then, adjust the drag so it slips before the line breaks.

How to Fight a Fish

PUMP the rod by lifting the handle firmly. Keep the rod tip high, while maintaining steady pressure until the fish begins to give ground.

REEL quickly while dropping the rod tip, but do not lower the rod so fast that the line goes slack. Pump and reel until the fish tires.

NEVER crank a spinning or spin-cast reel while the drag is slipping. Each turn of the handle puts a twist in the line, producing a snarled mess.

How to Land a Fish

NET fish headfirst. When the fish has tired, plunge the net into the water and lift quickly.

GAFF large fish only if they are to be kept. A gaff wound will most likely kill the fish.

GRAB largemouth and smallmouth bass by the lower lip. A tight grip seems to paralyze them.

The Gamefish

Largemouth Bass

Anglers from Canada to Cuba have marvelled at the explosive strike and breathtaking leaps of the largemouth bass. With its huge mouth open wide, a hooked largemouth takes to the air, shaking its head violently to throw the hook. Often it succeeds.

The largemouth has become the most widely-distributed gamefish in North America, partly because of its reputation as a fighter, but primarily because of its remarkable ability to survive in almost any freshwater lake, pond or stream. It thrives in pine-fringed lakes of southern Canada to murky backwaters in Illinois to sprawling desert reservoirs in Mexico.

Black bass, *bucketmouth* and *old linesides* are but a few names for the largemouth bass, which is actually a member of the sunfish family. Like sunfish and crappies, bass fan out shallow, saucer-shaped nests in the spring, usually in water 2 to 4 feet deep. Most spawning grounds are in bays, cuts or channels protected from the wind. Rough water can easily scatter eggs or destroy nests on windward shores.

Largemouth bass spawn when water warms to the low- to mid-60s. Bass in Florida usually deposit their eggs in February, while largemouths in Minnesota may not spawn until mid-June. After dropping her eggs, the female leaves the male to guard the eggs and the young until they can fend for themselves. Nest-guarding males may strike at almost anything that swims their way.

Typical bass foods are small fish, crayfish, frogs and insect larvae. The largemouth can adapt to almost any type of fresh water, because it eats a wide variety of foods. Snakes, turtles, mice and even birds have been found in bass stomachs.

The largemouth's size is determined by the length of the growing season. A trophy bass in Vermont might weigh 6 pounds, while 12-pound bass are not uncommon in Florida's warm waters. Though generally smaller, northern bass live longer than largemouth bass in the South. The world-record largemouth, caught in 1932, weighed 22 pounds, 4 ounces. It was caught in Montgomery Lake, Georgia. However, many experts believe the next world record will come from California, where several bass in the 20-pound range have been caught in recent years.

Largemouth Bass Range

SHALLOW WATER with a soft bottom and dense vegetation is typical habitat for largemouth bass. They prefer warm water, from 68° to 78°F, so they rarely go deeper than 20 feet. Bass lurk in the shade of weeds, where they can easily find baitfish, insects, frogs and other foods.

When to Catch Largemouth Bass

Largemouth bass tolerate more light than walleyes. Still, bass shy away from bright sunlight and are most active under dim conditions.

On sunny, summer days, bass feed at daybreak and dusk, spending midday along drop-offs close to feeding areas. Fishing is usually good on rainy or overcast days, but poor during and after a thunderstorm. Angling success declines in late summer when surface waters become too warm and bass foods become too abundant.

Fishing picks up again in fall when the shallows begin to cool. But when the water temperature drops to the low 50s, fewer bass are caught. In the North, largemouths rarely bite in late fall and winter.

Bass begin to feed heavily just prior to spawning in spring. Catching them is easy because nest-guarding males attack anything that comes near. Some states close bass fishing or prohibit angling in certain spawning areas until the nesting season is over.

Good Conditions for Fishing Bass

WARM DAYS in spring are good for catching largemouths. Best fishing is usually after two or more days of warm, sunny weather.

SPAWNING TIME finds male bass eager to strike. However, many anglers consider it unethical to catch bass on their spawning beds.

HEAVY RAIN or dark skies bring bass into the shallows to feed. But thunder will quickly scare them back into the depths.

Poor Conditions for Fishing Bass

FLAT CALM water and a sunny sky usually mean poor fishing. Calm mornings and evenings, however, may offer excellent surface-fishing.

STRONG WINDS drive bass into deeper water. They may continue to feed, but they will be scattered, making fishing difficult.

COLD FRONTS send bass into the depths. They become so inactive that divers have been able to swim up and touch them.

Where to Catch Largemouth Bass

Largemouth bass spend most of their lives in water that is only 5 to 15 feet deep, although sometimes they will move into deep water to find food or to escape sunlight.

Bass in the shallows are likely to be near some kind of shady cover, especially if the cover is near deep water. Natural and man-made features that attract largemouths include lily pads, hyacinth, overhanging trees, stumps, brush, bridge pilings and boat docks.

FARM PONDS can support surprisingly large numbers of bass. Most ponds are bulldozed, so their bottoms are featureless. Likely bass hangouts are cattail edges, flooded brush and beneath overhanging trees.

LILY PADS and other large-leaved weeds provide shade for largemouth bass. Anglers must use heavy monofilament to prevent bass from wrapping the line around the tough stems and breaking free.

DROP-OFFS along shorelines, around sunken islands or off tips of points attract bass, especially if the shallows have weedy cover.

OLD CREEK CHANNELS are outlined by flooded timber in many reservoirs. Bass feed in shallows, but can easily move into the deeper channel.

WEEDLINES concentrate largemouths. Most of the bass in a large area may gather in a narrow strip along the edge of a weedbed.

The Plastic Worm:
Number One Bass Producer

Plastic worms catch more bass than any other lure. They are most effective when the water temperature exceeds 65°F. They are not the best choice for fishing bass when the water is cold.

Originally introduced in the 1950s, plastic worms began catching so many bass that one southern state introduced legislation to have them banned. One reason for their effectiveness is that they can be fished in weedy and snag-filled water. When rigged Texas-style with a weedless slip-sinker, worms can be fished in the heaviest cover without hanging up. Under these conditions, anglers should use a stiff rod, a bait-casting reel and 15- to 20-pound test line.

Worms come in an amazing variety of colors, shapes, sizes and consistencies. Most anglers prefer black or dark colors when fishing murky water or in clear water when light is dim. Pale green is good on clear days in clear water. Purple is the most popular color for a variety of conditions.

How to Rig a Worm Texas-Style

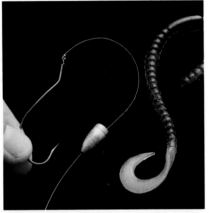

THREAD a small, cone-shaped sinker onto the line. Next, tie a worm hook to the line.

INSERT the hook into the worm's head, then thread the first half-inch of the worm onto the hook.

PUSH the hook through, give it a half twist and reinsert so the point barely sticks out.

How to Fish a Plastic Worm

RETRIEVE the worm by using a jigging motion (page 68). Work the worm through heavy cover such as weeds, brush or logs. The worm will rarely snag because the hook is concealed.

WATCH the line and rod tip. The line will twitch as the bass inhales the worm. Bass will usually strike while the worm is falling. Polaroid glasses help make the line more visible.

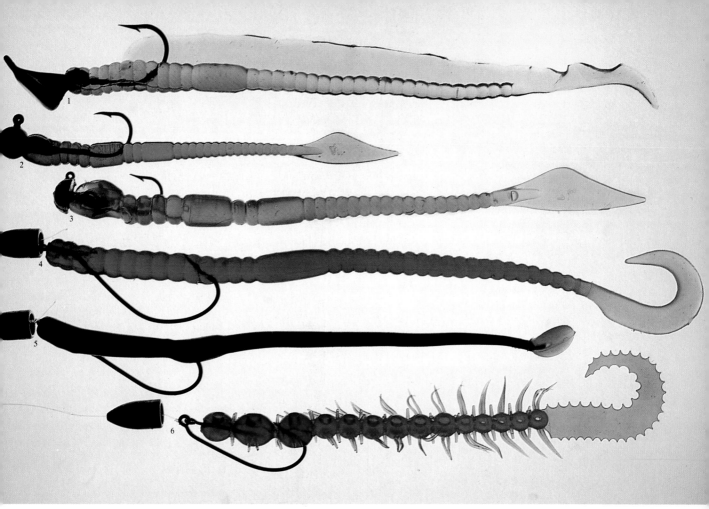

POPULAR RIGS for fishing plastic worms include (1) Pow'r head jig, used when fishing in heavy weeds; (2 and 3) ball type and mushroom heads, used on clean, hard bottoms; (4, 5 and 6) worm hooks used for Texas-style rigging. Worm bodies are interchangeable with different hooks and heads.

POINT the rod tip in the direction of the strike. Some fishermen prefer to wait a few seconds for the bass to swallow the worm, though most experts set the hook almost immediately.

SET the hook with a powerful sweeping motion. Driving the hook through a plastic worm and into the mouth of a bass requires more force than is normally used to set the hook on other fish.

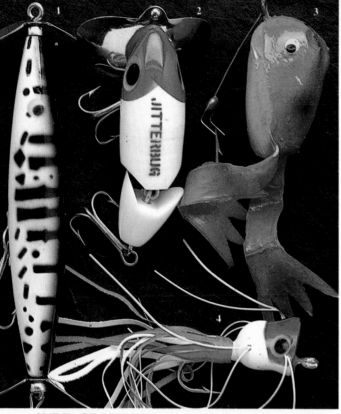

SURFACE LURES for largemouths include (1) Dying Flutter, (2) jointed Jitterbug, (3) Super Frog, (4) fly rod Hula Popper.

Surface Lures: For Exciting Action

Surface lures work best on calm summer mornings and evenings or on moonlit nights. They are less effective when wind ripples the water. Some surface lures have a built-in action and should be reeled back steadily. Others are designed to produce popping or chugging sounds when retrieved with sharp jerks followed by pauses.

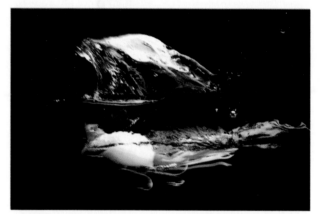

POPPERS should be cast over a suspected bass lie, then allowed to rest until the ripples are gone. Retrieve by alternately twitching and resting the popper.

Crankbaits: For Summertime Bass

Crankbaits include a wide variety of diving and vibrating lures. Some imitate natural foods, while others resemble nothing in the diet of bass. A bass strikes the latter type because it is annoyed by the noise, or because it sees the lure as a threat to its territory. Crankbait fishermen log their biggest catches in summer when bass are most active.

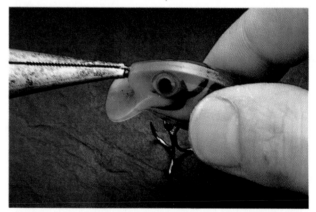

TUNING a crankbait makes it run in a straight line. If it begins to veer to one side, bend the eyelet slightly to the opposite side. A crankbait that is out-of-tune tips on its side and runs too close to the surface.

CRANKBAITS include (1) Big-O, (2) Bomber, (3) Mini Rattle Trap, (4) Young's Shad with interchangeable lip. The longer the lip, the deeper a crankbait runs.

Jigs: For Bass in Cool Water

Jigs or jig-minnow combinations catch largemouth bass in any season, but work best when water is cool and bass refuse fast-moving lures. Jigs should be retrieved slowly and with a hopping motion. Bass strike jigs lightly. Often, a slight tap is the only indication that a bass has inhaled the lure. A sensitive rod and light line are a must.

RUBBER-SKIRTED jigs are a good choice for bass in cool water. When jigged vertically, the action of the live-rubber skirt attracts bass.

JIGS for largemouth bass include (1) Black Hairy Worm, (2) weedless living rubber jig, (3) Dingo, (4) Mister Twister, (5) marabou.

Spinnerbaits: For Any Season

Spinnerbaits are the best, all-season lures for largemouth bass. They are especially effective in spring, when bass are in weedy shallows. Most are virtually snagless, so they can be tossed into dense weedbeds, brush or timber without hanging up. Spinnerbaits can also be fished along dropoffs and in water as deep as 20 feet.

MULTIPLE EXPOSURE photo shows drop-and-flutter motion used when retrieving a spinnerbait. Reel slowly, then pause while raising and lowering the rod tip. Reel again to take up slack line, then repeat the technique.

SPINNERBAITS for bass include (1) Buzz Bullet, (2) Tinsel Tail. To attract finicky largemouths, add a minnow to the hook.

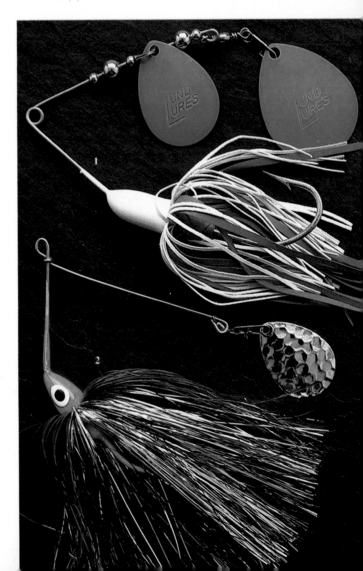

Smallmouth Bass

Wherever the water is cool and crayfish dart among rocks and boulders, fishermen are likely to find smallmouth bass. And, whenever the angler hooks a smallmouth, he is bound to see spectacular leaps and determination unrivaled among freshwater fish.

The thrill of battling a *bronzeback* was not available to many fishermen in years past. Prior to 1900, smallmouth bass were found mainly in the Great Lakes and in river systems in the east-central United States. But as the railroads moved west and north, smallmouths were stocked in many rivers, natural lakes and large reservoirs. Probably the most successful introduction was in the clear, rocky lakes of the southern Canadian Shield.

The smallmouth bass is a close cousin of the large-mouth, though the species differ in many ways. Smallmouths, for example, prefer slightly cooler water. They are most active in water 67° to 72°F and spawn in water from the upper 50s to lower 60s. While smallmouths spawn in cooler water, they may deposit their eggs a few days later than largemouths. The reason is that shallow, weedy bays used by spawning largemouths warm faster in spring than do the deeper, rocky sites preferred by smallmouth.

The diets of both species are somewhat similar. They feed on small fish, insects, frogs and worms. However, if crayfish are present, they are certain to be the smallmouth's favorite food.

Smallmouths do not reach the size of largemouth bass. A 5-pound smallmouth is considered a trophy in most waters, though many 7- to 8-pound bass are caught each year in Tennessee Valley Authority reservoirs in Kentucky, Tennessee and Alabama. The world record, caught in Dale Hollow Reservoir, Tennessee in 1955, weighed 11 pounds, 15 ounces.

Smallmouth Bass Range

SMALLMOUTH BASS have copper, dark brown or olive-green sides with vertical bars. The jaw extends only to the middle of the eye.

LARGEMOUTH BASS have a dark, horizontal band along the midline from gill to tail. The jaw extends beyond the eye.

Where to Catch Smallmouths in Lakes

POINTS attract smallmouth bass in natural lakes and reservoirs. Look for long, sand-gravel points with bulrushes, or gradually-tapering points made up of golfball- to baseball-sized rock.

Smallmouth bass lakes have one thing in common. They all have at least some rocky bottom to provide spawning habitat for bass. Cool, northern lakes have the largest smallmouth populations, although the biggest fish are caught in deep southern reservoirs such as those created by the Tennessee Valley Authority.

Most of the smallmouth's life is spent in 5 to 15 feet of water. They lurk in the shallows because most of their foods are there and because their eyes are not overly-sensitive to bright sunlight. In southern reservoirs, mid-summer heat may drive them into 30- to 40-foot depths during midday, though they return to the shallows to feed at dusk.

Smallmouth bass have well-defined territories. Once the fisherman finds a good spot, he may have to change angling methods with the seasons, but he seldom has to move far to find the fish.

FALLEN TREES are often the only source of overhead cover in rock-bound lakes with little vegetation. Smallmouth bass often crowd under trees for shade, so precise casting is a must.

ROCKY ISLANDS, either submerged or exposed, are excellent smallmouth spots in Canadian Shield lakes. Those surrounded by shallow water are better than islands that jut up sharply from the depths.

Where to Catch Smallmouths in Rivers

Coolwater streams with moderate current and rocky bottoms are favorite smallmouth haunts. Rarely do they live in warm, muddy streams.

River smallmouths prowl rocky shoals to find food. They seldom are found over flat, sandy bottoms. Although they may feed in fairly fast current, smallmouths spend most of their time in slack water. They lie near breaks in the current where fast and calm water are separated. Eddies below points, rocks or bridge abutments are favorite hangouts. Often they gather just downstream of trees that have toppled into the water.

Unlike lake-dwelling smallmouths, those in rivers rarely form large schools. Instead, a fish picks out a quiet spot behind rocks or logs where it lives with one or two other bass. When one is caught, another moves in to take its place. As a result, prime spots always hold bass, despite heavy fishing pressure.

SUBMERGED WINGDAMS (arrows) are built to deflect the current. In morning and evening, smallmouth bass feed in the shallows on top of the wingdams, but spend the day in the scour hole *above* the wingdam.

LARGE BOULDERS, logs and other obstructions break the current, creating a downstream eddy. While most smallmouths lie in the pocket below the obstruction, a few lie on the upstream side.

POINT BARS, where the current sweeps past the tip to form a downstream eddy, are excellent habitat for river smallmouth. They lie in slack water, then dart into the current to grab food.

Casting:
Number One Smallmouth Technique

Smallmouth bass, noted for their aggressive nature, will usually strike a lure cast into their territory. Still, small lures seem to work best. In spring, spinners and shallow-running lures resembling minnows are effective. In summer, when bass are deep, many anglers use lures that are crayfish look-alikes. Deep-diving crankbaits and jigs with rubber legs are among the favorites. Tail-spin lures can reach bass in water 20 feet or deeper.

Surface lures take many smallmouths, but should be fished differently than when casting for largemouths. Twitch the line gently, so the lure makes only a slight disturbance. Sharp pops or chugs seem to frighten smallmouths. Plugs with propellers at one or both ends are popular for surface fishing.

LURES for smallmouth bass include (1) floating Rapala, (2) Baby Big-O crankbait, (3) Ugly Bug, (4) Mister Twister, (5) Vibrax Spinner, (6) Tinsel Tail jig.

SLIPPING is a way to slow or stall a boat when fishing a river. By running the motor against the current, the angler has more time to cast toward likely spots and to work the lure deeper.

TARGET CASTING, placing a lure within inches of cover, is essential when bass are holding tight behind rocks or under trees. Often, they refuse to chase a lure unless it invades their territory.

Live Bait:
Best for Big Smallmouth

Sometimes, smallmouth bass will refuse to strike even the most expertly-placed lures. Then, a struggling frog, squirming leech or nightcrawler, shiner minnow, or live crayfish may be the answer. Live-bait fishing is often the only way to fool trophy smallmouths who are particular about what they eat.

A leech is an excellent smallmouth bait, especially when fishing around large rocks or boulders. Cast it close to the boulders, then either let it lie on bottom or retrieve it very slowly. Although smallmouths find them irresistible, crayfish are difficult to use. When still-fished on bottom, they crawl under rocks or sticks. The best method is to retrieve them slowly along bottom with a split-shot rig (page 69).

LIVE BAIT RIGS for bass include (1) crayfish with #4 hook, (2) leopard frog with #4 hook, (3) shiner minnow with #6 hook.

Fly-fishing:
For Smallmouths in the Shallows

Fly-casting is an exciting method for catching smallmouth bass. They tend to hold tight to cover, sometimes in areas nearly impossible to reach with spinning tackle. However, a good fly fisherman can cast to within inches of a smallmouth lie or carefully drift the lure enticingly close to a bass.

In spring, just before they move onto spawning beds, smallmouths eagerly strike artificial flies, bugs and poppers. Fly-fishing can also be good in summer, especially on calm mornings and evenings when insects are hatching. Streamer flies work best when bass are feeding on minnows in the shallows or in tails of pools.

FLY-FISHING LURES include (1) deer hair bass bug, (2) popper with live-rubber skirt, (3) marabou streamer, (4) Wooly Worm, (5) Muddler Minnow.

White Bass & Stripers

When a school of white bass churns the surface in pursuit of baitfish, there is no faster fishing. They instantly strike any lure cast into their midst. Fishing for striped bass can be just as exciting. Though schools are not as large, these trophy fish can put up a fight that rivals any other gamefish.

White bass, often called *silver bass*, have long been a favorite of freshwater fishermen. They are found in big rivers and connected lakes, and in large reser-

voirs. Striped bass, also called *rockfish* or *stripers*, were originally caught only in the ocean or in major coastal rivers during their spring spawning runs. However, when South Carolina's Santee and Cooper Rivers were dammed in 1941, striped bass were trapped above the dam. By 1950, stripers were thriving in Santee-Cooper Reservoir and fishermen were enjoying an exciting new sportfish. The success of stripers in Santee-Cooper Reservoir led to stocking programs in many other states and to development of the *whiterock*, a white bass-striper hybrid that has been introduced in many southern reservoirs.

Close cousins, white bass and stripers have similar lifestyles. Both species migrate up rivers and

streams in spring, spawning when the water temperature reaches about 58°F. Similarly, they both prefer large, open waters that have an abundance of gizzard or threadfin shad, their primary food.

White bass rarely exceed 3 pounds, while stripers often weigh more than 20 pounds. The record white bass, caught in the Colorado River, Texas in 1977, weighed 5 pounds, 9 ounces. The largest striper taken from inland waters was caught in Lake Havasu, Arizona in 1977. It weighed 59 pounds, 12 ounces.

White & Striped Bass
Combined Range

WHITE BASS have a flatter body than stripers (top photo). Lines on white bass tend to be lighter and more broken than those on striped bass and usually fall short of the tail. On stripers, lines extend from the gills to the tail.

When and Where to Catch
White Bass and Stripers

White bass and stripers are constantly on the move. A school of hungry bass may appear out of nowhere, providing fantastic fishing for several minutes, and then disappear just as quickly.

Huge schools of white bass and stripers migrate upstream in spring, stopping in pools and eddies along the way. They move upriver until a dam, waterfall or other obstruction blocks their progress.

After spawning, both species retreat downstream where they scatter in the open water of lakes or reservoirs. They spend most of the summer in water from 20 to 40 feet deep. At daybreak and dusk, they move onto shallow sand flats to chase schools of shad or shiners.

In late summer and fall, white bass and stripers slash into schools of shad. Bass may suddenly begin feeding at any time of day. Gulls diving to catch injured shad reveal the location of feeding bass. During calm weather, fishermen look for swirls on the surface or shad leaping above water to escape.

In the North, late fall and winter fishing is slow because bass rarely feed in water cooler than 50°F. However, in the deep South, they continue to feed through the winter months.

CIRCLING GULLS pinpoint the location of white and striped bass feeding on schools of shad. Binoculars are helpful for spotting gulls. Watch for them wheeling and diving to grab shad that bass chase to the surface. Get to

TAILWATERS below dams offer excellent white bass and striper fishing in spring. Fish congregate in eddies or slack water near fast current, where they feed on shiners and other small baitfish.

WHITE BASS (above) and stripers roam open water in large schools. Unlike most freshwater fish, they feed in packs, surrounding shad in open water, or herding them along shorelines or into dead-end bays.

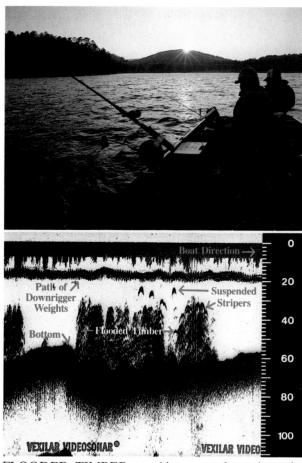

the spot quickly, because the action may be over within minutes if other boats spook the fish. Stop short of the school and drift within casting distance. If there is no wind, use an electric motor or oars.

FLOODED TIMBER provides cover for stripers in many reservoirs. This graph tape shows several stripers suspended just above the treetops. The downrigger weights can be seen tracking above the fish.

SHAD are super-abundant in many reservoirs. They form dense schools and feed on bits of algae and other tiny organisms near the surface. By late summer, shad are large enough to attract white bass and stripers.

WARMWATER DISCHARGES from power plants may attract millions of shad during winter. The shad, in turn, draw schools of white bass, providing fast fishing for anglers willing to brave the elements.

How to Catch White Bass and Stripers

LURES for white bass include (1) Fat Rap, (2) Panther Martin spinner, (3) Pixee spoon, (4) Sassy Shad, (5) Mister Twister, (6) Super Sonic.

Methods for catching white and striped bass are quite similar, though the larger stripers demand tougher equipment and bigger lures. Recommended is 15- to 25-pound test line, a heavy-duty bait-casting or spinning reel and a stiff 6- to 7½-foot rod. For white bass, use an ultralight or light-action spinning rod with 4- to 8-pound test line.

Fishing tactics and locations change with the seasons. In spring, fishermen converge on rivers, usually below dams, where bass are spawning. When thousands of white bass jam their spawning grounds, they strike almost any bait or lure tossed their way, from minnows and jigs to strips of red yarn. Catching stripers is not as easy. Although many are caught on spoons, plugs or spinners, live or cut baits such as shad, herring, suckers and shiners usually work better at spawning time. Most anglers use slip-sinker rigs for bait-fishing, casting them into eddies and areas with slow current.

Tips for Catching White Bass and Stripers

A POPPING PLUG (arrow) with hooks removed can be tied ahead of a small jig to add casting weight and attract bass. Anglers can cast into surface-feeding fish from farther away, with less chance of spooking them.

VERTICAL JIGGING is a technique for fishing white bass and stripers in deep water. Anglers troll until they locate a school, then stop and jig with spoons or lead-head jigs straight below the boat.

In summer, fishermen troll for deep-running schools of white bass and stripers, often locating them with depth finders. White bass are seldom deeper than 40 feet, though stripers may suspend as deep as 70 feet. To reach these fish, anglers use heavy slip-sinkers or lead-core lines, though down-riggers (page 150), are becoming popular for striper fishing in many reservoirs. Minnow-like plugs and spoons are favorite trolling lures for white and striped bass, but there are days when stripers want nothing but live or cut baits. To rig a shad or herring for drifting or trolling, slice off the head with a slanted, downward cut. Then, rig the body with a harness consisting of two #1 or #2 hooks.

Beginning in late summer and through fall, anglers in lakes and reservoirs switch to a technique called *jump-fishing*. When a school of surface-feeding bass is located, fishermen race to the spot, casting into the school with surface plugs, spinners or jigs. The action lasts only a short time, then anglers must find another active school. Sometimes jump-fishing results in a limit catch in a matter of minutes. Some fishermen rig one rod with a surface plug and another with a jig or diving plug. If one fails to produce, they quickly switch to the other rig to avoid wasting time.

TWIN-JIG set-ups can improve the white bass angler's success. Where legal, fishermen tie a three-way swivel onto 8-pound test line. Then, they add different lengths of 10- to 12-pound test, each with a small jig.

LURES for striped bass include (1) bucktail jig with twister tail, (2) Spoonbill Rebel, (3) Hellbender, (4) Tinsel Tail jig, (5) T-Spoon, (6) King Spot.

Bluegills

Bluegills offer something for everyone. For a youngster learning to fish, they are easy to catch. For the expert, catching big bluegills is a challenge. For the angler interested in sport, they put up the best fight for their size. And for those who enjoy a sweet-tasting fish, bluegills are unsurpassed. No wonder they are so popular.

Known in the South as *bream*, bluegills are members of the sunfish family. They are named for the distinctive, powdery-blue coloring on the lower part of the gill cover. Bluegills are also marked by a black gill flap and a dark spot at the rear base of the dorsal fin.

Spawning starts in spring when the water warms to about 68°F. Bluegills build spawning beds on sand or gravel bottoms in water 2 to 4 feet deep. Spawning continues for six weeks or more. Male bluegills guarding a nest attack anything that comes near, including a fisherman's bait.

The bluegill's diet includes insects, insect larvae, crustaceans and occasionally, small fish. They rarely eat minnows. In the North, bluegills eat several times their own body weight from May to October, but eat very little the rest of the year. Cold water makes them sluggish. In winter, they bite only on small baits.

Despite heavy fishing pressure, bluegills often overpopulate a lake because they produce millions of young. This results in too much competition for food and a slow growth rate. Under these conditions, none of the fish attain large size. The biggest bluegills are caught in southern waters and in lakes and ponds throughout the North with relatively low bluegill populations. The world record, 4 pounds, 12 ounces, was caught in Ketona Lake, Alabama in 1950.

Bluegill Range

PONDWEEDS are good cover and a source of food. Thick pondweed beds hide bluegills from predators and attract insects, crustaceans and other food organisms.

Where to Catch Bluegills

The best bluegill waters are moderately-fertile lakes, river backwaters, farm ponds and shallow reservoirs with some weed growth.

Shallow water holds bluegills from spring to early summer. As summer progresses, small bluegills remain in the shallows, but larger fish move to water as deep as 20 feet. Anglers looking for big bluegills during summer often fail to fish deep enough.

Lakes with dense weeds generally produce stunted fish. Young bluegills use the heavy cover to escape predators, so more fish survive to compete for the available food supply. Faced with this situation, a fisherman seeking large bluegills should find another lake with fewer weeds.

SPAWNING BEDS are light, dish-shaped depressions in the shallows. Catching spawners does not harm the population because bluegills produce so many young.

BULRUSH TIPS give a clue to bluegill location in early spring. Fish often move into sun-warmed shallows about the same time bulrushes appear above water.

DOCKS AND PIERS offer shade and protection from predators. They are favorite spots for bluegills on sunny days. Large bluegills prefer docks and piers near drop-offs.

SUSPENDED BLUEGILLS are sometimes found 8 to 12 feet down in 15 to 30 feet of water, especially on hot summer days. In morning and evening, they come into the shallows to feed for short periods.

FISHING BRIDGES concentrate bluegills by providing shade and by attracting various types of food. Bluegills are not easily spooked by fishing activity and often feed just below anglers' feet.

How to Catch Bluegills

Bobber fishing with live bait, such as worms, night-crawlers or small leeches, probably accounts for more bluegills than any other method. However, tiny artificial lures fished with ultralight tackle can be just as effective.

When fishing with a bobber, use 2- to 6-pound test line with a #8 hook. About 10 inches from the hook, add enough split-shot so the bobber barely floats. The bait should be 1 to 3 feet off the bottom. Alternately jiggle the bobber; then let it rest. Most bites come after the bait stops moving.

Bluegills do not school tightly, but will congregate in and around cover. When one is caught, it pays to work the surrounding area for more.

WORMS are the favorite bait of many bluegill anglers. Hook them several times so that only the ends dangle. Nibbling bluegills quickly steal a lightly hooked worm.

TWISTER-TAIL jigs in small sizes are popular lures for bluegills. Bounce them along bottom near the edge of a weedbed or retrieve them slowly above a bed of pondweed.

CANE POLES are ideal for fishing in thick cover. They enable the angler to drop the bait into hard-to-reach pockets and lift fish out vertically without tangling in weeds.

SMALL POPPERS catch bluegills on their spawning beds or when they are feeding on the surface. Retrieve with light twitches, allowing them to rest briefly after each twitch.

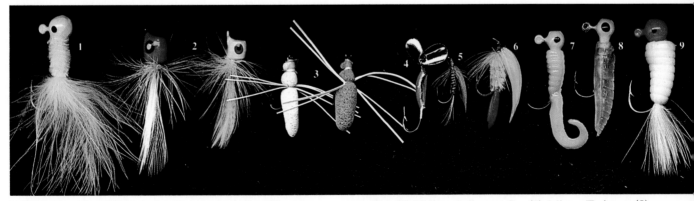

LURES for bluegills include (1) marabou jig, (2) poppers, (3) sponge spiders, (4) teardrop jig, (5) Ginger Quill wet fly, (6) Yellow Sally wet fly, (7) Mister Twister, (8) Tweetle Bug, (9) Fuzzy Grub.

Crappies

Crappies attract crowds of fishermen wherever they are found. Although they do not leap or make powerful runs like some fish, they are easy to catch and good to eat.

Like ruffed grouse and snowshoe hares, crappies undergo population cycles. They can be extremely abundant for a few years, and then mysteriously disappear. No one knows for sure why this happens.

Although crappies begin to congregate near spawning areas in early spring, spawning does not begin until the water reaches about 64°F. Like other members of the sunfish family, males guard the nest until the fry are old enough to leave.

Black crappies are more abundant in the North; white crappies prevail in the South. However, their ranges overlap considerably. White crappies are often found in turbid lakes; black crappies require clearer water.

Crappies are one of the prettiest fish in fresh water. Anglers have given them more than 50 colorful names including *calico bass, speckled bass, strawberry bass, papermouth* and *bachelor perch.*

Black & White Crappie
Combined Range

BLACK CRAPPIES have irregular dark speckles across the sides. The dorsal fin has seven or more spines. The world-record black crappie, 6 pounds, was caught in Westwego Canal, Louisiana in 1969.

WHITE CRAPPIES have dark speckles set in vertical bars. Dorsal spines usually number less than seven. The world-record white crappie, 5 pounds, 3 ounces, was caught in Enid Reservoir, Mississippi in 1957.

When and Where to Catch Crappies

Crappies occur in nearly every state and in many waters of southern Canada. They live in most warm-water lakes and in the slow-moving stretches of warm rivers and streams. White crappies prefer mud bottoms with lots of sunken brush, trees and other underwater cover. Black crappies favor hard bottoms and abundant vegetation.

Although crappies are usually found near some type of structure or cover, they sometimes roam open water in search of food. Finding them can be difficult because they may suspend over the deepest part of a lake.

Crappies feed both day and night, though prime feeding time is around dusk. During the spring spawning period, nest-guarding males can be caught throughout the day.

Like bluegills, crappies tend to overpopulate many waters causing the fish to become stunted. Anglers seeking big crappies should fish waters where the population is relatively low.

BULRUSH BEDS are good places to find crappies in spring. The shallow water, firm bottom and cover provide ideal spawning habitat.

SUSPENDED crappies may be found in open water far from shore. Find them by drifting, slow trolling or scouting with a depth finder.

NIGHT FISHING works well for crappies in clear lakes. Lights on docks or in boats draw insects and minnows that attract crappies.

FLOODED BRUSH concentrates crappies. Fishermen sometimes sink their own brush piles, though this requires a permit in some states.

SHALLOW BAYS warm quickly in early spring. On sunny days, crappies move from the main lake to school in water only a few feet deep.

DROP-OFFS are favorite midday haunts for black crappies. After feeding in shallow weedbeds in morning, they retreat to deeper water nearby.

How to Catch Crappies

Most crappies are caught on minnows or lures that resemble minnows. A slow, erratic retrieve is best, although crappies occasionally strike fast-moving lures. Twitching the lure, then allowing it to settle back, entices stubborn crappies to bite. They are likely to grab the lure as it falls.

Choice of lures depends on the depth of the crappies. Jigs and small, deep-diving plugs are good for deep water. When crappies are shallow, use floating-diving plugs, spoons or spinners.

The *countdown* method is used when casting jigs for suspended crappies. To find the right depth, cast the jig, then count as it sinks. After several seconds, begin the retrieve. Vary the count on successive casts until a crappie strikes, then stay with that count.

Light tackle is popular among crappie fishermen. Most use 2- to 6-pound test line, but 12- to 20-pound test may be necessary when fishing in thick cover, such as stumps or brush piles. If a bobber is used, it should be small enough so a crappie can pull it down easily.

The crappie nickname, papermouth, is derived from the paper-thin membrane around its mouth. Once a crappie is hooked, do not reset the hook or pump the rod. While these techniques may be necessary for other gamefish, they could tear the hook from the crappie's mouth.

HOOK minnows according to the angling technique. For bobber-fishing, hook the minnow behind the dorsal fin. When trolling, hook it through the lips. For jigging, hook the minnow in the head or through the eye sockets.

CRAPPIE LURES are small, ranging in length from 1 to 2 inches. Popular jigs are (1) marabous, (2) Mister Twisters, (3) Fuzzy Grubs. Any of these colorful jigs can be tipped with small minnows or tiny strips of pork rind as added enticements. Other popular lures include (4) fly rod spoon, (5) Mepps spinner, (6) Panther Martin spinner, (7) Rapala, (8) Teeny-R. To cast these small lures, use a flexible, ultralight rod.

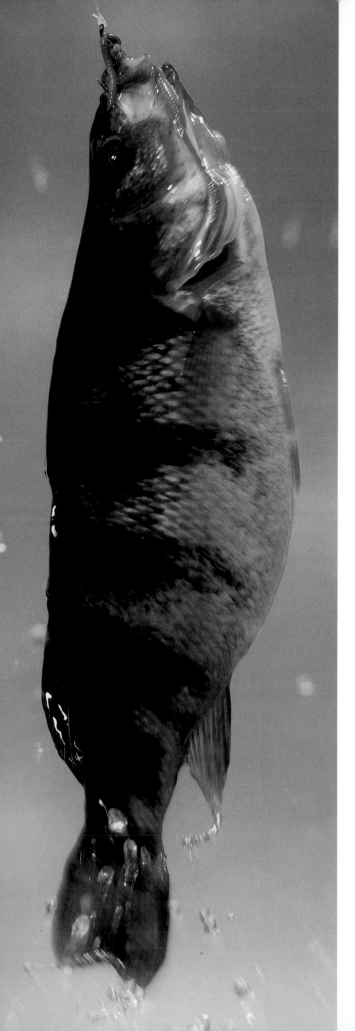

Perch

Perch are popular with fishermen, simply because they are among the tastiest of freshwater fish.

Closely related to walleyes and saugers, perch live in many of the same lakes and rivers, although they rarely become abundant in extremely murky waters. The largest populations are in clear, northern lakes with moderate vegetation. Perch have been stocked in many southern waters.

Perch feed only during the day, because they cannot see well in dim light. In the evening, schools break up and the fish rest on bottom. The next morning, they regroup into large schools which feed in open water. In some lakes and reservoirs they forage along shore. They are active throughout the year, even when the water is near freezing. In the North, perch are a favorite of ice fishermen.

Perch normally have yellow to yellow-green sides with about seven vertical bars. In some waters, their bodies are tinted gray or brown. Spawning males have more intense colors with orange or bright red lower fins.

Spawning occurs in spring when the water reaches about 45°F. Perch lay their eggs in jelly-like bands that cling to rocks, plants and debris on the bottom. Staggering numbers of young are hatched, much to the benefit of predators such as largemouth bass, northern pike and walleyes. Because their reproductive potential is so great, perch can withstand heavy fishing pressure. Commercial fishermen on Lake Erie have taken as many as 30 million pounds in a single year. In many waters, perch become too abundant and, as a result, never reach a size large enough to interest anglers. A 7- to 8-inch perch is an acceptable size to most anglers, though sometimes perch grow much larger. The world record, 4 pounds, 3½ ounces, was caught near Bordentown, New Jersey in 1865.

Perch
Range

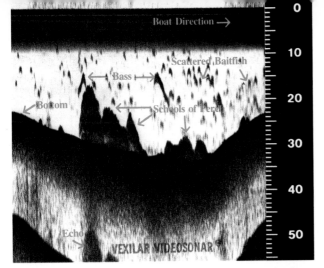

DEEP WATER usually holds more large perch than shallow water. This graph tape shows schools of large perch from 20 to 30 feet deep. The fish are packed together so tightly, they appear as solid masses on the tape.

PERCH BAITS include, left to right, worms, grub, strip of perch belly meat, crayfish tail and minnow. Perch are notorious bait thieves, so set the hook shortly after feeling a nibble.

Popular Bottom Rigs

SPINNER-WORM combinations are used when slow-trolling for perch. Use a fluorescent spinner blade and add enough split-shot, 8 to 12 inches from the hook, to keep the rig bumping along the bottom.

JIG-MINNOW setups work best when fished slowly. One of the best techniques is to bounce a one-eighth-ounce jig along bottom, straight below a slow-drifting boat. Plastic-bodied jigs work well for perch.

BELL SINKER rigs are made with one or more 3-way swivels, each with a short leader spliced into the line.

Catfish

Anyone who has battled a monstrous catfish or dined on fresh catfish fillets, knows why these be-whiskered fish have such a loyal following.

Flathead and blue catfish often exceed 50 pounds and many topping 100 pounds have been recorded, but not officially documented. Channel catfish weighing more than 20 pounds are seldom caught, though some big rivers produce much larger fish.

Channels and flatheads are the most common catfish species. Blue catfish populations are declining in many areas, but huge blues are caught in some parts of the central and southern United States. The smaller white catfish are confined mainly to the East and West Coasts. Other members of the catfish family include several types of bullheads and mad-toms. Also called *willow cats*, some madtom species are popular bait for walleyes and smallmouth bass.

Although catfish prefer warm water, some cool northern rivers have large populations. Catfish can tolerate extremely muddy water and even moderately high levels of pollution. However, unlike bullheads, catfish cannot live in waters prone to winterkill.

Catfish Combined Range

Catfish spawn in late spring when the water reaches about 70°F. They have a curious habit of spawning in enclosed areas such as muskrat runs and other holes in riverbanks, sunken barrels or hollow logs.

CHANNEL CATFISH (above) and blue catfish have forked tails. Blues have 30 to 35 anal fin rays, and channels 24 to 29. The world-record blue, 97 pounds, was caught in the Missouri River, South Dakota in 1959. The record channel cat, 58 pounds, was taken in Santee-Cooper Reservoir, South Carolina in 1964.

FLATHEAD CATFISH, also called mud or yellow cats, have flat heads, protruding lower jaws, mottled brownish sides and rounded tails that are usually slightly notched. The anal fin has about 16 rays. The world-record flathead, 79 pounds, 8 ounces, was caught in the White River, Indiana in 1966.

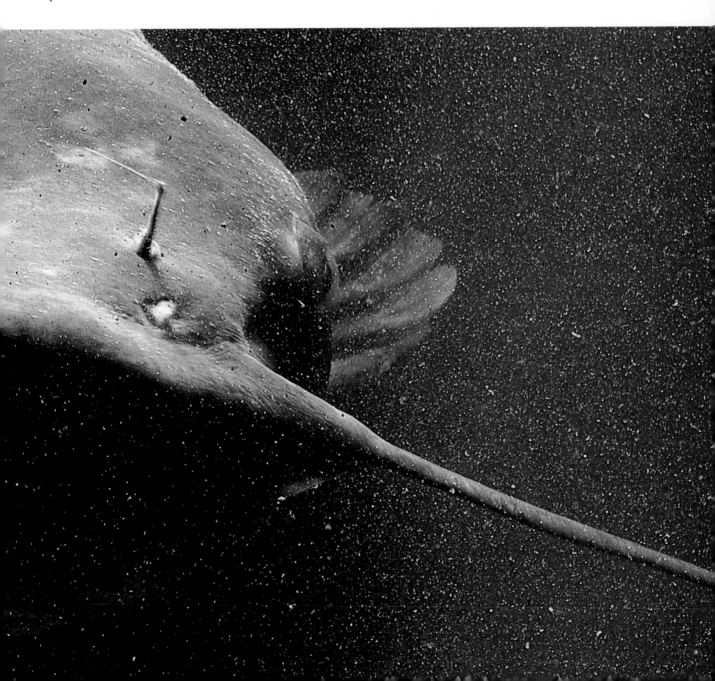

When and Where to Catch Catfish

NIGHT FISHING is effective because catfish do not rely on their eyes to find food. Instead, they detect and identify potential foods with sensitive taste buds that cover their whisker-like barbels.

Catfish bite best at night, but can be caught during the day, especially after a heavy rain when river levels are rising. Then, even midday fishing can be good. Catfishing slacks off when the water temperature drops below 55°F. At temperatures below 40°F, they do not feed. In larger northern rivers, catfish form huge schools during winter and remain almost motionless in deep water.

Catfish are primarily river fish. They also live in reservoirs and lakes connected to rivers, and have been stocked extensively in lakes and ponds throughout much of the United States.

Flathead and channel catfish prefer similar habitats, though flatheads tend to be loners. Both species like rivers with slow to moderate current, deep pools, plenty of downed timber and sunken logs for cover and hard bottoms of sand, gravel and rubble. Catfish live in the deep pools during the day, then move into shallower feeding areas after dark. Blue catfish prefer faster water, often living in swift chutes or pools with noticeable current.

Typical Catfish Habitat

STOCKED PONDS are common in the southern United States. Many are harvested commercially, though some are stocked for sport fishing.

DEEP POOLS below large dams are resting and feeding areas for larger catfish. Cats bite day or night in these turbulent waters.

LOG-STREWN CHANNELS, with deep holes and a combination of slow and fast currents, are prime catfish spots in many rivers.

How to Catch Catfish

STILL-FISHING gear includes a forked stick for propping up the rod and a bell (inset) clipped onto the rod tip to signal a bite at night. Be sure to leave the bail open or the spool free.

Almost anything goes when it comes to catfish baits. The list includes soap, congealed chicken blood, entrails of small animals, freshwater clams that have rotted in the sun for a day or two, dead birds, mice, frogs, worms, crayfish, grasshoppers, Limburger cheese, doughballs and any number of homemade or commercially produced stinkbaits. Live or dead fish, especially those with high oil content such as gizzard shad and smelt, are effective because they give off a scent that carries a long distance.

Whatever the bait, it should be fished on bottom. Catfish swim slowly, groping with their barbels to find food. Suspended baits are usually ignored.

Catfish anglers do not need sophisticated equipment, but it should be strong. For fishing around snags and rocks, 20- to 50-pound test line is best. Heavy tackle can turn a big catfish, preventing it from wrapping the line around a log and breaking free. In tailraces with strong current, up to a pound of weight may be needed to keep the bait on bottom and prevent it from drifting.

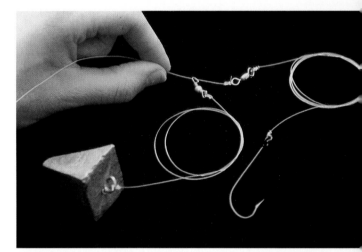

BOTTOM-FISHING rigs can be made with a pyramid sinker to hold the bait in place. The sinker is attached to a short length of monofilament tied to a barrel swivel that slides like a slip-sinker.

Popular Catfish Baits

BLUE AND CHANNEL CATS prefer cut fish, worms or baits that give off a strong smell, such as cheeses or stinkbaits. However, they occasionally take live minnows and even artificial lures such as spinners.

FLATHEAD CATFISH are caught almost exclusively on live fish, though a dead fish rigged so it flutters in the current can be effective. Baitfish weighing up to 2 pounds are used for big flatheads.

Bullheads

Bullheads are popular simply because they are abundant and easy to catch. An old lawn chair, a cane pole and a can of angleworms are all a fisherman needs to fill a gunnysack with bullheads.

Three species of bullheads, black, brown and yellow, are caught by fishermen. Black bullheads seldom grow larger than 1 pound, yet this species boasts the largest world record bullhead, an 8-pounder caught in Lake Waccabuc, New York in 1951. Yellow bullheads frequently grow larger than blacks, although the world record is smaller, only 3 pounds, 3 ounces. It was caught in Nelson Lake, Wisconsin in 1972. The world-record brown bullhead, 5 pounds, 8 ounces, was taken from Veal Pond, Georgia in 1975.

Prime time for bullhead fishing is late spring and summer, after the water temperature has warmed above 60°F. Bullheads may feed anytime during the day, but become more active toward evening when they cruise the shallows for insect larvae, snails, worms, fish eggs and small fish. Bullheads also eat a variety of aquatic plants.

Warm waters of shallow lakes, rivers, marshes and ponds may become over-crowded with stunted bullheads. In winterkill lakes, bullheads often outlast other fish species, because they require only minute amounts of oxygen. Bullheads have been known to survive in lakes that freeze almost to the bottom by simply burrowing several inches into the soft ooze.

Bullheads are delicious to eat if caught during spring and early summer, but as the water warms, their flesh softens and may develop a muddy taste. Fishermen should be extremely careful when handling or cleaning bullheads, because their venom-coated spines can inflict a painful wound.

Bullhead
Combined Range

MUDDY WATERS of slow-moving rivers, shallow lakes or ponds are favorite bullhead spots. Black bullheads tolerate the muddiest water; browns and yellows prefer clearer water with more weeds.

LATE EVENING or nighttime is best for bullhead fishing. Like catfish, bullheads have little trouble finding food in the dark. They rely on an acute sense of smell, plus taste buds in their barbels.

BAITS for bullheads are similar to those used for catfish. Included are (1) doughballs concocted from flour, Parmesan cheese and water, (2) chicken liver, (3) soft plastic worm smeared with stinkbait and threaded with a line and small treble hook, (4) gob of worms on a long-shanked hook, (5) cotton ball soaked with blood, (6) cheese ball. Other proven baits are nightcrawlers, live or dead minnows and chunks of laundry soap.

How to Handle Bullheads

GRIP a bullhead firmly, because its skin is slippery. Carefully position the fingers and thumb to avoid the sharp dorsal and pectoral spines (arrows).

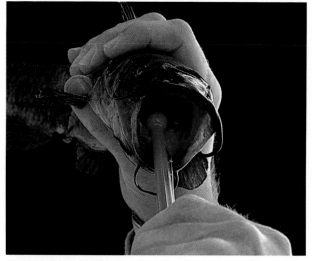

UNHOOK a bullhead using a hook disgorger (above) or longnose pliers. Bullheads have powerful jaws, so anglers should not attempt to remove hooks with their fingers.

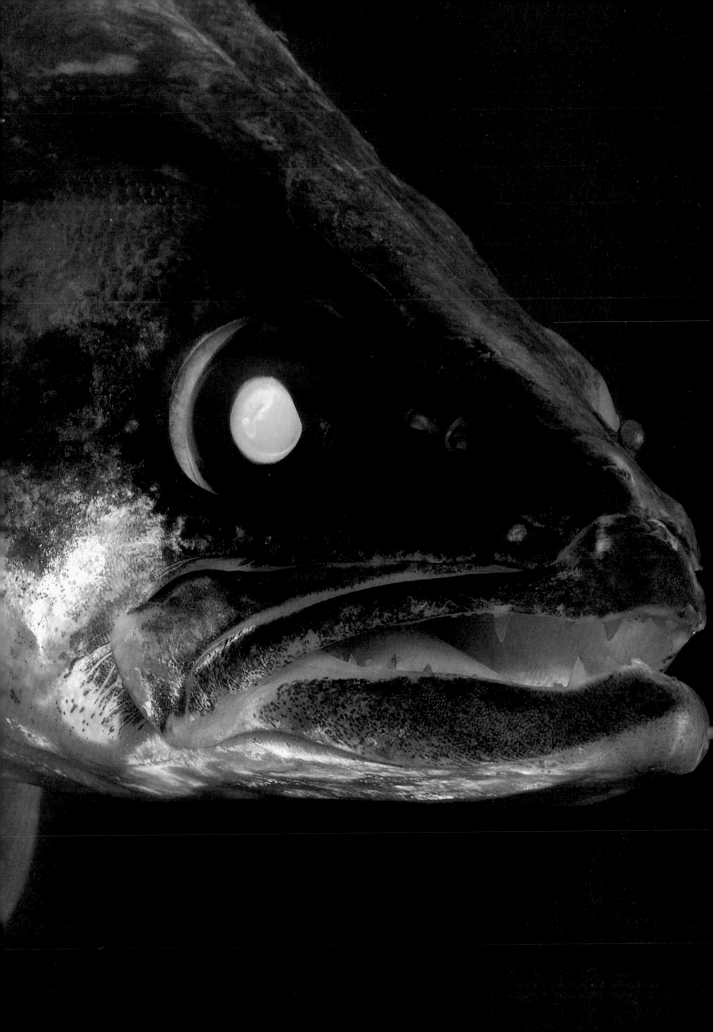

Walleyes

Walleyes are creatures of darkness. Like deer, owls and many other animals that are active at night, they have a layer of pigment in the retina of the eye called the *Tapetum lucidum*. This light-sensitive layer forces them to seek murky or dimly-lit water, a fact important to fishermen.

Many anglers mistakenly refer to walleyes as walleyed pike. They actually belong to the perch family, which also includes saugers and yellow perch.

Walleyes and saugers may inhabit the same waters, though saugers are primarily a river species. Because the two are quite similar in appearance, fishermen are often confused as to which species is on their stringer. Distinguishing marks are the white tip on the lower part of the walleye's tail and the rows of black spots on the sauger's dorsal fin.

Because of their popularity in north-central states and Canada, walleyes have been stocked along the Atlantic Seaboard and throughout the western states, as well as in some areas of Canada where they were not native.

Walleyes are coolwater fish. In summer, for example, they are usually found in water from 60° to 70°F. Spawning begins in spring when the water warms to about 48°F, which means early March in the South to mid-May in northern climates. Fishing for female walleyes is poor during spawning and remains slow for another 10 days thereafter, until the fish can recuperate. But the smaller males often continue to bite. After spawning, walleyes go on a month-long feeding binge.

Although some walleyes survive longer than 20 years, most live 10 years or less. In Northern waters, where they grow more slowly, it will take about 6 years for a walleye to reach 2 pounds and an 8-pound fish is considered a trophy. In southern reservoirs, walleyes will quite often reach 2 pounds in only 3 to 4 years and fishermen catch 15- to 20-pound fish each year. The world-record walleye, 25 pounds, was caught in Old Hickory Lake, Tennessee in 1960.

Walleye
Range

NIGHT VISION makes the walleye an efficient predator. It prowls the shallows after nightfall, eating young perch, shiners, shad and other fish that cannot see as well and make no attempt to escape.

SCHOOLS of walleyes usually lie close to the bottom, but occasionally suspend much higher. Sometimes, hundreds of walleyes are packed into a school only 20 to 30 feet in diameter.

When to Catch Walleyes

Walleye fishing peaks when foods are least abundant. The food supply is lowest in spring, when most of the previous year's baitfish have been eaten, and a new crop has yet to be produced.

Yellow perch and most other baitfish spawn in the spring, but the young do not reach a size attractive to walleyes until mid-summer. When 2- to 3-inch perch become plentiful, walleyes have no trouble finding food and become harder to catch.

Toward fall, when much of the current year's baitfish supply has been eaten, walleyes must spend more time searching the shallows for food. So, even though walleyes may consume more food in mid-summer, fishing is best in spring and fall.

LATE EVENING or early morning are the best times to catch walleyes in clear lakes. At midday, their shallow feeding grounds become too bright, and walleyes edge into deep water where they feed very little.

CLOUDY OR WINDY conditions improve daytime walleye fishing in clear lakes. A choppy surface scatters the sun's rays, reducing light penetration. Under these conditions, walleyes may remain in the shallows all day.

DECREASING LIGHT triggers walleye feeding. As a result, one of the best times to catch them is just before a thunderstorm.

DAYTIME is best for fishing walleyes in lakes and rivers where murky water screens out sunlight. Night fishing in these waters is usually poor.

AVOID fishing clear lakes on bright, calm afternoons. Under these conditions, walleyes feed mainly at night, often in water less than 5 feet deep.

Where to Catch Walleyes

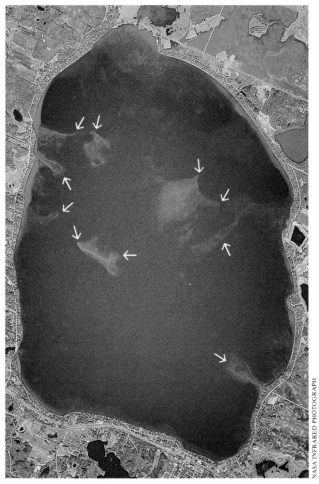

DROP-OFFS concentrate walleyes. Check a contour map for sunken islands, points or bars. Arrows on this high-altitude photograph pinpoint areas most likely to hold walleyes during summer.

Walleyes shift location as the seasons change. In spring, they remain in warm shallows for several weeks after spawning, usually in water 15 feet or less. They can stay in the shallows all day, because the low angle of the sun's rays has little effect on their light-sensitive eyes.

As summer approaches, the shallows become too warm and the sun rises higher in the sky, forcing walleyes to retreat to cooler depths. However, they move shallower to feed in morning and evening.

In summer, walleyes generally remain in the upper portion of the thermocline where the water is slightly cooler than the surface. Rarely do they go deeper than 30 feet.

In fall, walleyes return to the shallows as the surface begins to cool. Once again, the sun has fallen low on the horizon, so the fish can feed in shallow water all day. Walleyes start to scatter when fall turnover begins. By the time the surface temperature drops to the low 40s, they may be as deep as 50 feet.

Oxygen content also affects the location of walleyes. In summer, many fertile lakes lack oxygen in the depths, so walleyes are forced to remain in the shallows, often at depths of 10 feet or less.

SAND bottoms appeal to walleyes in the spring after they spawn. Try fishing along the sandy, outside edges of bulrush beds.

ROCK or gravel bottoms attract walleyes. Crevices in the rocks hide insects and their larvae, crustaceans and other walleye foods.

AVOID soft, mucky bottoms because they seldom support walleye foods. If the anchor shows traces of mud, move to another spot.

Trolling: A Basic Walleye Technique

LONG-LINE TROLLING is a good way to fish shallow water without spooking walleyes. A shallow-running lure

DEEP TROLLING works best with a snag-resistant bottom-walker (above), a bell sinker or a sinker that can be

SLIP-SINKER trolling is ideal for fussy walleyes. The line slips freely through the sinker, so the fish can run with little resistance. Use the lightest sinker that will keep the

Trolling is the best fishing strategy when walleyes are scattered. Many anglers troll until they find a school of walleyes, then throw out a marker and switch to another technique, such as jigging or slip-bobber fishing. Either method allows the angler to cover a small area thoroughly.

Live bait must be trolled slowly. Many fishermen back troll (page 66) for walleyes. By operating the motor in reverse, the boat can be slowed to a crawl. Back-trolling also offers better boat control on windy days. Slip-sinker rigs with live baits are commonly used when back-trolling. Because walleyes grab slow-trolled baits so lightly, fishermen must develop a sensitive touch or they will fail to detect a high percentage of bites.

Popular baits for trolling are shiner minnows, leeches and nightcrawlers. Minnows work best in spring and fall when the water is cold. Crawlers and leeches catch more walleyes in summer. When angling for large walleyes, some fishermen prefer 5- to 6-inch chubs or shiners, or small salamanders.

Artificial lures should be trolled faster than live baits. Sometimes a fast-moving plug will trigger a strike when a slow-moving lure is ignored.

How to Rig and Fish a Slip-Sinker

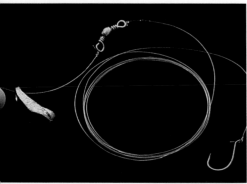

THREAD on a sinker and tie on a swivel. Add a leader with a #4 or #6 hook to the other end of the swivel.

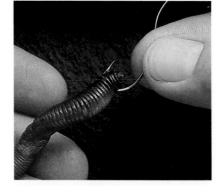

HOOK a nightcrawler through the head, a leech above the sucker or a minnow through the lips.

TROLL with the bail open. Keep one finger on the line while pulling the sinker slowly along the bottom.

is trolled 100 to 150 feet behind the boat. By the time a walleye sees the lure, the boat is far beyond.

pinched or twisted onto the line. As the water gets deeper, let out more line or use a heavier sinker.

bait close to the bottom. A 2- to 4-foot leader is used when fish are near bottom. A longer leader with a small float is needed for suspended walleyes.

TROLLING LURES for walleyes include (1) jointed Rapala, (2) Flatfish, (3) Rebel, (4) Lindy Baitfish, (5) spinner rig used with live bait, (6) Thinfin.

BITES are subtle. Walleyes swim off slowly after picking up the bait, leaving the sinker to rest on the bottom.

RELEASE the line at the slightest tug. Let it flow freely off the spool until the walleye stops running.

POINT the rod tip at the fish. Quickly reel up the slack until feeling resistance. Set the hook with a sharp snap.

The Slip-bobber: For Suspended Walleyes

Walleyes sometimes suspend several feet off bottom, especially in mid-summer. There, they are difficult to catch by standard fishing methods. Bottom rigs place the bait too deep. Bobber rigs set at 10 feet or more are impossible to cast because of too much dangling line. A slip-bobber, however, makes it possible to cast with ease and place the bait at any level. Try different depths until a walleye strikes.

How the Slip-bobber Works

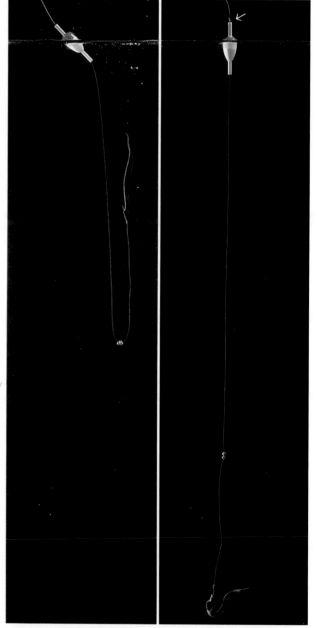

TO RIG the slip-bobber, tie a knot on the line at the desired depth. Thread on the bobber and add split-shot for balance. Tie on a #6 hook and bait with a leech.

LINE SLIPS through the bobber until the knot (arrow) stops the bait at the right depth. The weight of the sinker will then tip the bobber upright.

Casting:
For Walleyes in the Shallows

Shuffling of tackle boxes or the chugging of an outboard motor spook walleyes in shallow water. When
casting from a boat, stay as far as possible from the
feeding area to reduce the chances of scaring fish.
Casting at night is sometimes the only way to catch
walleyes in clear lakes. They spend the day in deep
water, but after dark, move onto shallow shoals where
they are caught on minnow-like plugs.

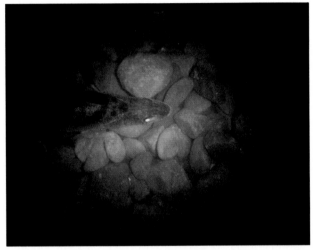

SPOTLIGHTS can be used to locate walleyes in the
shallows at night. Their eyes reflect the beam much like
the eyes of a cat reflect the headlights of a car.

LURES for casting include (1) Mepps spinner, (2) Erie
Dearie, used with or without live bait, (3) Tippy live bait
rig, (4) floating Rapala, (5) Super Sonic.

Jigging:
Another Basic Walleye Technique

Lead head jigs are most effective in murky lakes or
rivers where visibility is poor. Walleyes in these
waters are conditioned to strike quickly or risk los-
ing a meal.

River fishermen cast jigs along current breaks or
into eddies where the current is slow. Another technique is to anchor just upstream of a wingdam, cast
toward the dam, then slowly retrieve the jig.

Lake fishermen work jigs along drop-offs, weedbeds
and tips of points. Jigs with weedguards are good in
heavy cover. Jig-minnow combinations usually out-
fish plain jigs in both lakes and rivers.

WALLEYE JIGS include (1) Mister Twister, (2) feather
jig, (3) Sassy Shad, (4) Fuzzy Grub, (5) bucktail. Many
walleye fishermen favor yellow jigs.

Northern Pike

With its snake-like body, huge head and razor-sharp teeth, the northern pike has a fearsome appearance and a reputation to match. It is not uncommon for a pike to strike a large bass or walleye struggling on a fisherman's line. In some instances, pike have re-

fused to let go, even as they were guided into a landing net.

In North America, three members of the pike family are of interest to fishermen. They include the northern pike, muskellunge and chain pickerel. Grass and redfin pickerel are caught occasionally, but they rarely exceed 12 inches in length.

Known regionally as *jack, pickerel* or *snake,* northern pike are found across the northern United States and into Canada. They have also been stocked in waters as far south as Texas. In some areas of Alaska and Canada, pike are considered rough fish and fishermen kill them rather than return them to the water. But wherever they exist in

the United States, northerns are extremely popular with fishermen.

Lakes with shallow, weedy bays or connecting marshes are ideal for pike. Northerns spawn soon after ice-out, beginning when the water reaches about 40°F. They scatter their eggs onto dense vegetation in shallow bays or marshes. They refuse to bite just before and during spawning, but begin feeding actively soon after.

In most waters, northern pike reign supreme. They may feed on muskrats, mice, turtles, salamanders, small ducks and other birds, though most of their food is fish. Often they strike fish one-half their body length.

Pike are persistent. They sometimes follow a lure, hitting it repeatedly until hooked. Because they are easily caught, large northerns can be readily skimmed off a population. Today, most pike weighing over 20 pounds are taken in remote northern lakes and rivers where fishing pressure is light. The world-record northern pike, 46 pounds, 2 ounces, was caught in Sacandaga Reservoir, New York in 1940. However, many larger pike have been caught by fishermen in Scotland, Ireland and Germany.

Northern Pike
Range

When and Where to Catch Northern Pike

Locating small northern pike is easy. They spend nearly all of their time in shallow, weedy water from 2 to 15 feet deep. But finding big northerns is not as simple. They are found along with small pike in spring, but when the shallows warm in summer, they move into 15- to 30-foot depths. Fishing becomes more difficult because the big pike are scattered. Summer angling is also difficult if the water becomes too warm. If pike cannot find water cooler than 75°F, they eat very little.

Northerns bite best during daylight hours. Night fishing is seldom worthwhile.

Mature northerns tend to stay in one spot, usually hiding in weedy cover. Typically, a northern lies motionless in the weeds or alongside a log, where it can make short lunges at passing fish.

The northern pike is one of the most adaptable fish species. As shown in the photos below, they live in nearly every type of freshwater environment.

GREAT LAKES' BAYS concentrate large numbers of pike. The bays offer warmer water and more food than the open waters of the main lake.

SHALLOW RESERVOIRS often produce large northerns. Most pike are found in weedy cover, though flooded timber holds a few fish.

WEEDY BAYS of large lakes hold northerns most of the year. Pike lie near weedlines or in small pockets within weedbeds.

BACKWATERS of large rivers are haunts for northern pike. Those with deep areas adjacent to shallow weedbeds have the most fish.

CANADIAN SHIELD lakes can grow trophy northerns, provided that fishing pressure is light enough for pike to survive and grow.

MARSHES are too shallow for most gamefish and are prone to winterkill. Pike can usually survive because they tolerate low oxygen levels.

Bobber Fishing for Northerns

A northern cannot resist a big minnow dangling from a bobber. Though a pike may stare at the struggling baitfish for a long time, sooner or later it curls its body into a Z and then attacks. All the angler has to do is cast the bobber rig near a likely weedline, drop-off, sunken island or point, then sit back and wait.

If large minnows are not available at a local bait shop, some anglers head for the nearest creek to catch their own suckers, chubs or redhorse.

FIGHTING a big pike tests the angler's tackle and skill. Often, a northern puts up little resistance until several feet from the boat. Then, without warning, it makes a strong run, its tail churning the water surface.

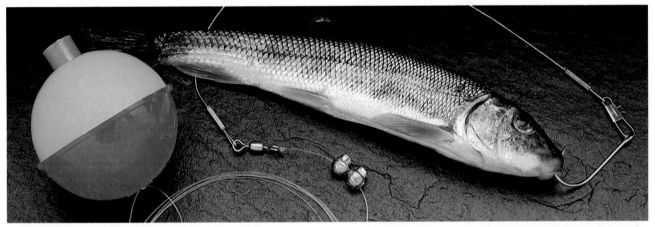

BOBBER RIGS are made with a 12-inch steel leader and a #1 or 1/0 hook. Attach a 1½- to 2-inch diameter bobber to the line. Add sinkers or split-shot for balance. Hook a large minnow in the upper lip or behind the dorsal fin. A variety of baitfish are used for still-fishing, including suckers, perch, chubs, shiners, ciscoes and whitefish. Whatever the species, the baitfish should measure 6 to 12 inches in length and be fresh and lively.

THE STRIKE of a large northern pike is often violent. The fish may yank the bobber so hard that it makes a splash as it is pulled under.

RELEASE line after the strike. A pike often grabs a minnow crosswise and runs with it. Then, it stops to swallow the bait headfirst.

SET the hook only after the pike has stopped. Reel in slack line until feeling the fish's weight. Then, snap the rod hard to sink the hook.

Speed Trolling:
High Speed Action for Pike

Trolling at high speeds imparts a furious action to lures, triggering strikes from northerns that pass up slow-moving lures.

Speed trolling works best in summer, after pike have left the shallows and retreated to deeper weedbeds. Unlike most angling techniques, speed trolling seems to catch more pike during the hottest and brightest hours of the day.

Fishermen troll just off weedlines, usually in 10 to 20 feet of water, with wide-lipped, deep-diving plugs that track straight at high speeds. Most anglers use stiff trolling rods, heavy-duty level-wind reels and metered monofilament line, from 20- to 25-pound test. Metered line makes it easier to keep the lure at a consistent depth.

HIGH SPEEDS are essential to successful speed trolling. The lures should have a frenzied action, which is not possible at slower speeds. Most anglers are hesitant to troll fast enough to make the technique work.

Casting:
When Pike Prowl the Shallows

Casting enables the angler to fish water that is too weedy, shallow or snag-infested for trolling. It is most successful in spring and fall, when northerns spend much of their time in shallow water.

Tackle must be fairly heavy. Strong, short rods and 12- to 20-pound lines handle the stress from casting heavy lures. Northerns have extremely sharp teeth, so wire leaders should always be used.

Pike normally find food by sight, but also use their lateral line to sense the direction and speed of prey. As a result, lures with lively action work best. Metal spoons that wobble enticingly are all-time favorites. Bright colors, including red, yellow and silver, are most popular. Anglers vary the speed of the retrieve and occasionally pump the lure for extra action.

CASTING from a boat enables the fisherman to drop a lure in small pockets in weedbeds or to cast parallel to weedy edges, so the lure runs through prime territory over the length of the retrieve.

SHORE CASTING is effective in spring when large pike roam inshore waters. Shore fishermen catch northerns throughout the summer in lakes and rivers of the extreme northern United States and Canada.

LURES for northern pike include (1) Reaper, (2) Red Eye Wiggler, (3) Dardevle, (4) Pikie Minnow, (5) Fuzzy Grub, (6) Bomber, (7) Mepps spinner, (8) Rapala.

Muskellunge

Many fishermen regard the muskellunge as big game, a rare trophy that demands hours of patient searching and stalking. Even if the angler can get close to a muskie sunning in a quiet bay, he knows the fish is not likely to strike. A muskie routinely ignores lures passing within inches of its jaws. Or, it may follow a lure to the boat, give the fisherman a menacing glare, then slip back into the depths. But all the effort and frustration, all the hours of casting heavy lures and plugs, are suddenly forgotten once a big muskie is hooked.

Close relatives, muskies and northern pike are similar in appearance. Most muskies have dark bars or spots on a light body, although some are void of markings. Northern pike have light spots on a dark background. Northerns have scales on the lower half of their gills and cheeks; muskies do not. The two species have been successfully crossed to produce the *tiger muskie,* a hardy, fast-growing hybrid.

Northern pike and muskies share many of the same waters. However, pike almost always outnumber muskies, because their eggs hatch earlier and their offspring eat the smaller muskie fry. But given the chance to survive, a muskellunge will grow larger than a northern pike. Each year, anglers take many fish weighing over 35 pounds. The world record, 69 pounds, 15 ounces, was caught in the St. Lawrence River, New York in 1957.

Like northerns, muskies feed on a variety of fish, though almost anything that looks edible is fair

MUSKIE LURES are big, ranging in length from 8 to 14 inches. Popular types include bucktail spinners, jerk baits,

game. Muskies feed mainly at dawn and dusk, and occasionally at night. Most are caught during the hottest part of summer, but the largest fish are taken in fall. They bite best on overcast days.

Recent tagging studies have shown that muskies spend most of their time in deep water, often 30 feet or more. However, muskellunge are not active at these depths. Feeding muskies are generally found in large, weedy bays, around sunken islands topped with weeds or near flooded timber.

Muskie fishing requires heavy tackle. Because a muskie clamps down so hard on a lure, the angler must set the hook several times to break the fish's grip and to sink the barbs. Short, strong rods and heavy casting reels enable the fisherman to cast or troll over-sized lures. They also help turn a running muskie. Monofilament or braided dacron lines of

20- to 50-pound test are normally used. Steel leaders are necessary because of the muskie's sharp teeth.

Popular muskie lures feature flash, furious action or noise. Some lures, called *jerk baits*, have no built-in action. The fisherman simply jerks them through the water. Occasionally, a muskellunge will follow a lure to the boat several times, always turning away at the last moment. When this happens, the knowledgeable muskie fisherman plunges the rod tip into the water and quickly weaves the lure through a series of figure eights. Rather than scaring the fish, this last-ditch maneuver may trigger a strike.

Muskellunge Range

deep-running crankbaits and jointed plugs, such as this Pikie Minnow (shown actual size).

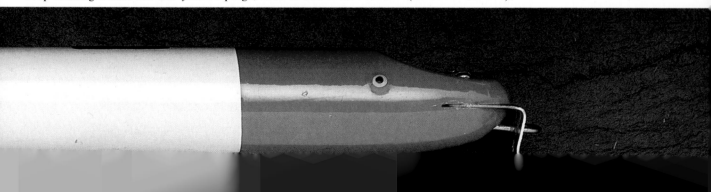

Trout

When fishermen think of trout, they picture a secluded mountain lake or spring-fed stream flowing through a woods. Surprisingly, most cold waters in North America, unless polluted, support some type of trout. These waters, however, do not have many other kinds of fish.

Fishermen pursue four major trout species in North America. Brook trout favor water of about 54°F, and are rarely found where the water temperature exceeds 65°F. As a result, they usually live in the upper reaches of streams or near the mouths of tributaries. Rainbows and cutthroats prefer water of about 55°F, but are found in waters up to 70°F. Brown trout favor water of about 65°F, but can tolerate temperatures as warm as 75°F. They some-

times live in warmer, slower-moving streams unsuitable to other trout.

Insects are the staple in the stream trout's diet. So, the best trout streams usually have the most insect life. Streams of lesser quality are often warmer and hatch fewer insects. Trout in such waters survive by eating mostly small fish. These streams have fewer trout, but are more likely to produce a trophy.

In addition to man, many kinds of birds, mammals, crustaceans, fish and even insects prey upon trout. To survive, trout must be cautious. Their hideouts are over-hanging vegetation, undercut banks, large rocks, fallen trees or deep pools. Large trout hooked in small streams are seldom landed. They are strong swimmers and once hooked, their first instinct is to dash for cover. A big trout may quickly wrap the line around a rock or other snag to break free.

Trout
Combined Range

RAINBOW TROUT are named for the pinkish band along their sides. Black spots cover the tail and flanks. Rainbows prefer swift water, but will abandon home streams to live in downstream lakes. They usually leap when hooked and put up an unforgettable fight. The world-record rainbow, 37 pounds, was caught in Lake Pend Oreille, Idaho in 1947.

BROWN TROUT, sometimes called *Loch Leven* trout, have backs and sides with black spots and sometimes a few orange spots with light halos. Tails may have a few scattered spots near the top, or none at all. Brown trout are the wariest and most difficult to catch. The world-record brown trout, 33 pounds, 10 ounces, was caught in Flaming Gorge Reservoir, Utah in 1977.

BROOK TROUT, often called speckled trout, have light spots on their sides and pale, worm-like markings on their backs. Leading edges of the lower fins have white borders. Brook trout are considered the easiest trout to catch and the best to eat. The world-record brook trout, 14 pounds, 8 ounces, was caught in the Nipigon River, Ontario in 1916.

CUTTHROAT TROUT are named for the reddish-orange slashes on both sides of the lower jaw. Like rainbows, their tails and sides are covered with black spots, though background color is more yellowish. Cutthroats prefer habitat similar to that of rainbows, but are mainly found in the West. Pyramid Lake, Nevada, yielded the world-record cutthroat, 41 pounds, in 1925.

ENEMIES of trout include fish-eating insects, such as this giant water beetle, plus otters, herons, kingfishers, loons and larger trout. Young trout must learn to be cautious or perish.

SNEAK up to the streambank and keep movement to a minimum. Study the water carefully to locate possible trout lies. Plan your fishing strategy before making the first cast.

WEAR drab colors, keep low and avoid open backgrounds. Because light rays bend at the water surface, trout can see all but the lowest objects along the streambank through the window (page 8).

Approaching Trout

Trout survive by being wary. Any sudden movement, shadow, noise or vibration will send them darting for cover. And once spooked, no amount of coaxing will get a trout to bite. If it is obvious that a trout has been disturbed, move on to another spot, because it may be awhile before the fish resumes feeding. Because trout are so skittish, the angler should take extra care when approaching a trout's lie and when presenting a lure.

WADING is the most common method of fishing trout in streams. Anglers should try to avoid scuffing the bottom, making large ripples and casting a shadow over the suspected lie of a trout.

When to Catch Trout

Trout can be caught almost anytime of the day or night, although they normally feed when light is dim. And with good reason. Insect activity peaks during evening hours, leaving the stream teeming with prime trout food.

Water temperature also affects feeding activity. In spring, trout are most active in the afternoon when the water is warmest. Later in summer, they feed in the early morning when the water is coolest.

Insects emerge from the stream bottom in cycles. Trout may go on a feeding frenzy during a large insect hatch, and catching them can be fairly easy. Some stream anglers work their way downstream, thinking that mud and insects they stir up make trout more likely to bite. However, not all fishermen agree with this strategy.

The largest trout are usually caught during peak feeding times. They keep smaller ones away from the best feeding spots. Small trout feed only after the large fish have eaten their fill and departed.

Rising water may be a good indication that trout are feeding. Rains wash insects and other foods off streambanks and over-hanging trees. As the stream rises and the current grows stronger, insect larvae and other morsels are dislodged from bottom. Trout begin feeding when the swirling water carries food past their lies.

MORNING AND EVENING, when sunlight strikes the water at a low angle, are peak feeding times. Fishing is usually slowest on lakes and streams during mid-afternoon, though fish may feed on a cloudy day.

NIGHTTIME is best for catching large brown trout, one of the wariest gamefish. Under cover of darkness, the angler can get closer to fish and use heavier lines and lures.

INSECT HATCHES may cause trout to gorge themselves on any food or bait drifting in the water. Or, they may be quite choosy. Then, only an exact imitation of the hatching insect will entice them to bite.

131

Stream Fishing:
Find the Feeding Areas

The number of trout living in a typical, coldwater stream would amaze most fishermen. Trout are seldom seen because they spend most of the day hiding. The only time they betray their presence is when they leave cover to find food.

Stream trout depend on the current to carry food to them. So, the best feeding areas are those places where the natural flow of water gathers food. Examples are eddies, deep holes below rapids or waterfalls and shallow riffles. On warm, sunny days, trout may lie near shaded streambanks, eating food that falls or washes into the stream.

Trout seek shade and cover beneath undercut banks and logs, below large rocks, or in deep pools. They do not feed actively in these resting areas, but will dart from cover to grab food as it drifts by.

Trout location may change during the year, depending upon water temperature. A stream with springs scattered along its course stays cold enough for trout all summer. But if spring-flow is confined to one section, the remainder of the stream may become too warm, concentrating the trout in water cooled by the springs.

LARGE STREAMS provide a variety of trout habitat. Trout lies in this high-altitude, infrared photo include (1) area below a tributary stream, (2) deep hole along an outside bend, (3) cut between islands, (4) shaded streambank, (5) long riffle, (6) eddy below a boulder.

COLDWATER DRAWS pull water from the bottom of a reservoir rather than from the surface, creating streams cold enough for trout. In the south-central United States, trout exceeding 20 pounds are sometimes caught in streams of this type.

Lake Fishing:
Find the Right Temperature

Trout thrive in a wide variety of coldwater basins, from small lakes and ponds to huge Lake Superior, the largest body of fresh water in the world. In some lakes, trout populations are continually replenished by reproduction in tributary streams. However, most trout lakes and reservoirs must be stocked.

Much of the year, trout remain near shore, feeding on minnows, insects and crustaceans. They sometimes school around food-rich inlets or near rock bars, sunken islands and points extending from shore. Their location, however, depends more on water temperature than on structure or bottom type.

During summer, trout may be forced deeper as the lake warms. They often squeeze into the narrow band of the thermocline because water below this point has too little oxygen. Although the surface water is warm, trout rise to feed on insects in early morning and late evening.

Compared to most gamefish, lake-dwelling trout are easy to catch. As a result, their numbers can be quickly reduced if fishing pressure is heavy. Best angling is in lightly-fished waters where trout can grow for several years before they are caught.

RESERVOIRS, especially those at high altitudes in the West, grow huge trout. Shorelines usually drop off sharply, so trout are found close to shore. The world-record brown trout was caught in a western reservoir.

PONDS need a permanent source of cold water to sustain trout. Often a large spring or artesian well is tapped to feed a series of man-made pools. Because water temperature in ponds is uniform, trout may be anywhere.

NATURAL LAKES in the northern United States and Canada or in mountainous regions sometimes have water cold enough to support trout. The fish normally cruise within casting distance of shore, although they may go deeper in summer.

GREAT LAKES trout, particularly rainbows and browns, concentrate near stream mouths, piers or discharges from power plants during spring and fall. In mid-summer, many trout are caught by trolling with downriggers in water 50 to 100 feet deep.

HOOK the bait so it moves naturally in the current. Hook worms through the collar, minnows in the head and nymphs and grasshoppers just behind the head. Be sure the bait is fresh and lively.

Bait Fishing: A Year-around Favorite

Fishing with natural baits probably catches more trout than any other method. In spring and early summer when streams are high and clouded by runoff, it may be the only way to catch trout, especially if few insects are hatching.

A long rod, 7 to 9 feet, makes it easier to swing or drop the bait into hard-to-reach places. Choice of line depends on water clarity. Four-pound monofilament is best in clear water where trout spook easily. Eight-pound test can be used in muddy water. Most fishermen use #8 short-shank hooks.

Many anglers gather bait along the stream. Worms, minnows, grasshoppers and nymphs are the most popular. When using small and fragile baits, set the hook as soon as the fish bites. Wait longer with larger baits.

LOB the bait to avoid tearing it off the hook. Using an easy sidearm motion, angle the cast across current and upstream. Keep the line tight as the bait bounces along bottom. Set the hook when the bait stops drifting.

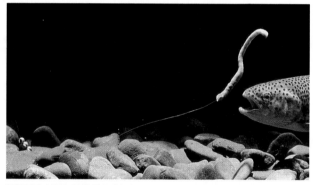

STREAM BOTTOMS produce most trout foods. Attach enough split-shot 8 to 10 inches above the hook to keep the bait near bottom. Too much weight keeps the bait from rolling with the current.

SPAWN works well in fall, winter and spring. Wrap it in a transparent nylon bag (page 154) or put a single egg on a hook. Trout instinctively respond to the color and smell of fresh spawn.

GROCERY BAITS, such as cheese, marshmallows and canned corn, are most effective on hatchery-reared trout. Wild trout prefer baits which more closely resemble natural foods.

Artificial Lures: For Big Trout

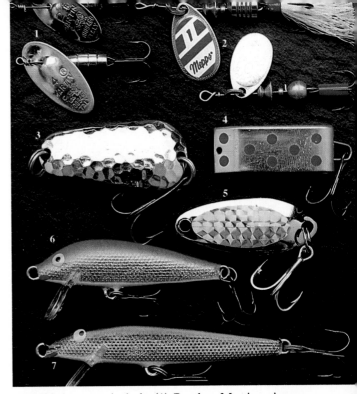

Most artificial lures resemble minnows and attract the larger, fish-eating trout. To imitate a swimming minnow, work the lure slowly along the bottom. A fast retrieve will sometimes provoke a reflex strike when a trout suddenly spots the flashing lure.

A delicate touch is not needed when fishing with artificials. Trout attack lures fiercely, usually hooking themselves. Some fishermen use lines as heavy as 12-pound monofilament to handle large fish and to retrieve snagged lures, but 8-pound test is usually strong enough.

An angler can cover a lot of water in a short time by casting an artificial lure. Trout that are feeding actively usually hit the lure immediately. If a few casts into a likely area fail to produce a strike, move on to another spot.

LURES for trout include (1) Panther Martin spinners, (2) Mepps spinners, (3) Wob-L-Rite spoon, (4) Super Duper, (5) Little Jewel spoon, (6) Countdown Rapala, (7) floating Rapala.

CAST the lure across current and upstream. Complete the retrieve before the line begins to bow downstream. Angle the cast farther upstream in faster current. This will eliminate downstream drag at the end of the retrieve.

FLIP the lure when casting into tight spots. Using a sharp, backhand motion, flick the lure under obstacles such as overhanging trees, bridges or logs across the stream. Try to keep the cast as low as possible.

RIFFLES hide actively-feeding fish. Cast the lure directly upstream and reel it back rapidly. Trout in the riffles often chase fast-moving foods.

SHORE CASTING with artificial lures in morning and evening catches trout cruising the shallows. Piers and stream mouths attract fish all day.

COWBELLS and other attractors draw trout to the bait or lure. They are especially effective when trolling for trout scattered in open water.

Fly-fishing:
For Warm Weather and Clear Water

Fly-fishing is not a mysterious art. The basic skills can be learned in a few hours. However, precision casting and a thorough knowledge of stream insect life take years of practice and study.

Artificial flies resemble specific items in a trout's diet, from tiny insect larvae to large minnows. Most flies fall into one of four basic categories:

DRY FLIES. Resembling newly-hatched insects, dry flies float lightly on the water surface. They have a fringe of delicate feathers or *hackle* near the head that keeps them afloat. They are tied with or without wings. Dry flies are rubbed with a waxy dressing or dipped in silicone to keep them buoyant.

WET FLIES. Tied with wings about the same length as the body, wet flies resemble a variety of trout foods, including immature aquatic insects, drowned land insects, crustaceans or minnows. They are retrieved below the surface. Hackles on wet flies are less prominent than on dry flies.

STREAMERS. Designed to imitate minnows, streamers are fished below the surface. The wings, made of feathers or hair, are longer than the body. Most streamers are brightly colored. Those made of hair are called *bucktails*.

NYMPHS. Although similar to wet flies, nymphs are tied without wings. They closely resemble many of the immature insects found in streams.

NYMPHS: (1) Light Hendrickson, (2) Emerging Caddis, (3) Bitch Creek, (4) Dark Hendrickson, (5) Caddis, (6) Light Cahill, (7) Wooly Worm, (8) Montana.
WET FLIES: (9) Black Gnat, (10) Ginger Quill, (11) Coachman, (12) Blue Dun, (13) Royal Coachman, (14) Dark Cahill.
DRY FLIES: (15) Pale Evening Dun, (16) Dark Cahill, (17) Gray Wulff, (18) Henryville Special, (19) Ginger

How to Fish a Dry Fly

CAST upstream, either straight or diagonally. Allow the fly to float naturally with the current. Strip in slack line, but take care not to drag the fly across the surface.

HACKLE keeps flies floating high on the water. It also creates a tiny depression which distorts the fly's image, so a trout is less likely to recognize it as a fake.

DRAG is the dry fly fisherman's biggest concern. If the fly floats faster or slower than the current, it leaves a wake that makes the fly appear unnatural to trout.

How to Fish Nymphs

CAST diagonally upstream, keeping the line tight as the nymph drifts along the bottom. Recognizing a strike can be difficult. Experts watch the fly line; then set the hook at the slightest twitch or hesitation.

NYMPHS imitate insect larvae that live on the lake or stream bottom. This multiple-exposure photograph shows a nymph being retrieved slowly along the bottom, as if it were rolling and drifting with the current.

Quill, (20) March Brown, (21) Adams, (22) Mosquito, (23) Royal Coachman, (24) Light Cahill, (25) Quill Gordon, (26) Ginger Bivisible, (27) Blue Dun.
STREAMERS: (28) Mickey Finn Mylar, (29) White-Orange Marion Marabou, (30) Muddler Minnow, (31) Royal Coachman, (32) Black Marabou Muddler, (33) Gray Ghost, (34) Supervisor, (35) Olive Matuka, (36) Integration Mylar.

How to Fish Wet Flies and Streamers

CAST across current when using a wet fly or streamer. For deeper water, angle the cast slightly upstream so the fly can sink longer before the current sweeps it downstream. More depth can be attained by using a sinking line, tiny split-shot or lead leader-wrap.

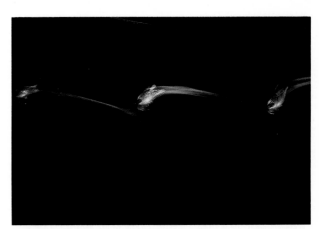

STREAMERS resemble baitfish darting through the water. Retrieve them in a jerky manner, as shown in this multiple-exposure photograph. Streamers are the largest of the artificial flies and they are normally used to catch larger trout.

137

Steelhead: The Sea-run Rainbow

The fighting ability of steelhead is legend. They have been clocked at 26.8 feet per second, fastest of any freshwater fish. A hooked steelhead will leap repeatedly, sometimes clearing the surface by 2 to 3 feet. Small wonder that even the best steelhead fishermen land few of the fish they hook.

Steelhead are rainbow trout that spend their adult lives at sea or in the open water of the Great Lakes. Each spring, they enter streams to spawn. Great Lakes tributaries have another, smaller run in fall, though no spawning takes place. Along the Pacific Coast, they may move into a stream in summer and remain until spawning time the following spring. Steelhead can be found somewhere along the Pacific Coast every month of the year.

Pacific Coast steelhead were introduced into the Great Lakes in the late 1800s. Runs have since developed in many streams, especially those with clean, cold water and gravel bottoms. Because non-migratory rainbows have also been stocked in the Great Lakes, fishermen sometimes mistake these deeper-bodied rainbows for steelhead.

Steelhead swim miles up tributary streams to find the right spawning area. They easily navigate raging cascades and most waterfalls. Only a dam or high waterfall blocks their progress. While in the stream, they bite reluctantly, ignoring baits drifted past them many times. When they suddenly decide to strike, they frequently catch the angler off-guard.

Steelhead generally grow larger than rainbows that live in streams. The average steelhead weighs 4 to 6 pounds, though some exceed 20 pounds. The world-record steelhead is 42 pounds, 2 ounces. It was caught at Bell Island, Alaska in 1970.

SPAWNING BEDS or redds may hold several steelhead. A female is sometimes accompanied by two or more smaller males.

WATERFALLS and dams block upstream migrations. Steelhead spawn in pools and runs from the stream mouth to the first impassable barrier.

STREAM MOUTHS are gathering spots for steelhead en route to upstream spawning grounds. The fish run when rain clouds the water.

How to Drift-fish for Steelhead

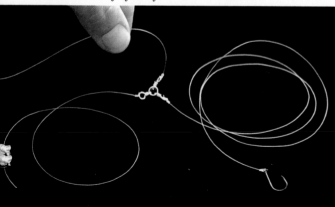

A DRIFT-FISHING RIG is made with a 3-way swivel. Tie an 8- to 10-pound dropper line to one eye and pinch on split-shot. Next, tie 20 to 30 inches of 12-pound line to another eye and attach a #4 or #6 hook.

SWING the bait upstream. Follow it with the rod tip as it drifts downstream. When it stops, set the hook. Good equipment for drift fishing is a 9-foot, heavy-action fly rod, a single-action reel and 12-pound monofilament.

THREE TYPES of rainbow trout are found in fresh water. Stream rainbows (top) have pronounced black spots on the back and sides with a distinct reddish band along the lateral line. Steelhead (middle) have sleek, silvery bodies with faint spots on the sides and back. As spawning time approaches, their bodies get darker and develop the characteristic red band. Lake rainbows (bottom) resemble steelhead, but have much deeper bodies.

BAITS AND LURES commonly used for drift-fishing include (1) spawn bags, (2) colored sponge balls, (3) Okie Drifter, (4) bulk yarn and finished yarn fly, (5) plastic salmon eggs. Spawn bags (page 154) probably take more steelhead than any other bait or artificial lure. Both trout and salmon spawn will attract steelhead. Yarn flies may be used alone or in combination with spawn bags or plastic salmon eggs.

Lake Trout

The prospect of battling a huge lake trout draws anglers to remote lakes as far north as the Arctic Circle. These waters yield many 30- to 40-pound lake trout each year. The sport fishing record, 65 pounds, was caught in Great Bear Lake, Northwest Territories in 1970. Even larger trout have been netted in Canadian waters, including a 102-pound giant caught in Saskatchewan's Lake Athabasca.

In parts of Canada, lake trout are known as *Mackinaw* or *gray trout*, although the most popular nickname is *laker*. Lake trout resemble brook trout, except the tails of lakers are deeply forked, while those of brook trout are nearly square. Lake trout in the Great Lakes are silvery-gray with white spots. Elsewhere, they have light spots on a background that may vary from dark green to brown or black.

Lake trout prefer water from 48° to 52°F, colder than any other gamefish. They will die if unable to find water under 65°F. During summer, lakers might descend to 200 feet in search of cold water.

Many lakes have water cold enough for lake trout, but lack oxygen in their depths. As a result, lakers are restricted mainly to the cold, sterile lakes of the Canadian Shield, the Great Lakes and deep, mountain lakes of the West.

Lakers grow slowly in these frigid waters. In some lakes of northern Canada, a 10-pound laker might be 20 years or older. The age of a trophy lake trout may exceed 40 years. Because they grow so slowly, they can be easily over-harvested.

Unlike most other trout species, lakers spawn in lakes rather than rivers. Spawning occurs in fall over a bottom of baseball- to football-sized rocks. Water depth varies considerably, but is usually 5 to 20 feet.

Lake trout have excellent vision. However, because so little light reaches the depths, they rely heavily on their sense of smell and their lateral line to find food. In some waters, they feed exclusively on aquatic insects, worms and crustaceans. In other lakes, lake trout eat only fish, mainly ciscoes, whitefish, sculpins and smelt.

Lake Trout Range

A lake trout, brook trout hybrid, called *splake*, has been stocked in some northern lakes, including Lake Huron. Splake mature earlier than lake trout and grow faster than either parent, so they are less affected by fishing pressure.

WILDERNESS WATERS, particularly those in Canada's Northwest Territories, provide excellent lake trout fishing. The lakes and rivers are so cold that anglers can use light tackle to catch lakers in shallow water through-out summer. Many of these lakes are ice-free only two to three months and can be reached only by airplane. As a result, fishing pressure is light enough for these waters to produce many trophy lakers.

When and Where to Catch Lake Trout

EARLY SPRING, beginning shortly after ice-out, offers the fastest lake trout fishing of the year. Lakers crowd into warmer water near shore, usually remaining in water 30 feet or less.

Water temperature plays a major role in the lives of lake trout. Following ice-out, the upper layer of a lake warms faster than water in the depths. Lake trout move from deep water into the warmer shallows where they remain for two to three weeks or until the water becomes too warm.

In summer, trout go as deep as necessary to find water near 50°F. In the Great Lakes or in lakes of the southern Canadian Shield, lakers may plunge to 100 feet or more. In lakes of extreme northern Canada, the shallows are always cold enough for lakers, so they remain in water 20 feet or less throughout summer.

In many deep lakes, trout school near bottom where water is in the low 40s. However, these fish are virtually impossible to catch. The catchable trout are likely to suspend in water 50 to 70 feet deep, darting into shallower water to grab unsuspecting ciscoes or other baitfish. Novice anglers often make the mistake of fishing for the more numerous, bottom-hugging trout, while ignoring lakers that are more prone to bite.

Lake trout move into much shallower water just before the fall spawning period. They are easily

Using a Recording Depth Finder for Lake Trout

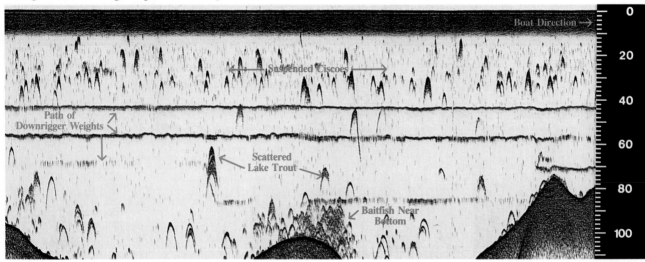

SUMMER finds lake trout in the depths. When trout are schooled in deep water, a recording depth finder is invaluable for locating the fish. This graph tape shows lake trout scattered from 40 feet to bottom. Above them, at 25 to 35 feet, is a dense band of ciscoes. Two lines are being trolled with downriggers through the shallower lake trout, the fish that are apt to bite. Another line is tracking through trout closer to the bottom.

caught on rocky reefs, sometimes in water only 5 feet deep. Because lake trout are so vulnerable, most states and provinces prohibit fishing during spawning time.

Regardless of the season, lake trout feed almost exclusively during the day, though shallow-water lakers feed when light is dim.

CANADIAN SHIELD lakes are ideally suited for lake trout. These coldwater, rocky basins are found mainly in the eastern half of Canada and the extreme northern United States, from Minnesota to Maine.

GREAT LAKES trout have made a remarkable comeback after they were nearly wiped out by the sea lamprey and commercial fishing. Lake trout populations have been rebuilt by lamprey control and restocking programs.

Springtime Lake Trout Spots

ROCKY POINTS often attract small lake trout to shallow water on top of the points, while larger fish remain in deeper water off the tips.

NASA INFRARED PHOTOGRAPH

NARROWS joining two large basins may become crowded with lake trout searching for warmer water. Anglers catch lakers as they pass through.

RIVER MOUTHS bring in warm meltwater which attracts lake trout. They are also drawn to schools of baitfish that hang around the plume.

143

Shallow-water Lake Trout Techniques

When lakers move into shallow water in spring and fall, the best methods are casting with flashy spoons or still-fishing with natural bait. A moving boat may spook lake trout in shallow water, so trolling is often not as productive unless anglers use trolling boards (page 151) or very long lines.

Lake trout shy away from heavy line, so clear, low-diameter line from 8- to 12-pound test is recommended. In clear lakes, some anglers use line as light as 4-pound test. Most fishermen prefer medium-action spinning tackle.

CASTING with heavy gold or silver spoons is a proven technique when lakers are concentrated off points, in narrows, along islands or over spawning reefs. Cast from a long distance away to prevent spooking the trout.

STILL-FISHING takes advantage of the lake trout's habit of scavenging dead fish off bottom. Cast a whole or cut fish on a slip-sinker rig. Prop up the rod and open the bail so the rod cannot be pulled into the lake.

NATURAL BAITS include smelt and strips of sucker meat. Some anglers combine a chunk of sucker with a live sucker or chub hooked through the lips. Only one hook is needed, because lakers quickly swallow the bait.

Deep-water Lake Trout Techniques

In years past, wire-line trolling was the standard procedure for catching lake trout in the depths. New equipment and techniques, however, make it possible to fish deep with much lighter tackle. Downrigger trolling (page 150), used to catch salmon in the Great Lakes, works just as well for lakers.

Deep lake trout are frequently scattered and sluggish, so adding an attractor, such as a dodger or cowbells, can improve the troller's success. Another light-tackle technique, vertical jigging, is becoming popular on Canadian Shield lakes.

HEAVY SINKERS, some weighing 8 ounces or more, are used for trolling in deep lakes. A short, stiff rod is needed to handle the heavy weight.

WIRE-LINE trolling, though it takes away much of a fish's fight, is still an efficient way to catch lake trout in deep water.

DIVING PLANES pull the line downward, but flatten out when a trout strikes, enabling the angler to play a fish with less resistance.

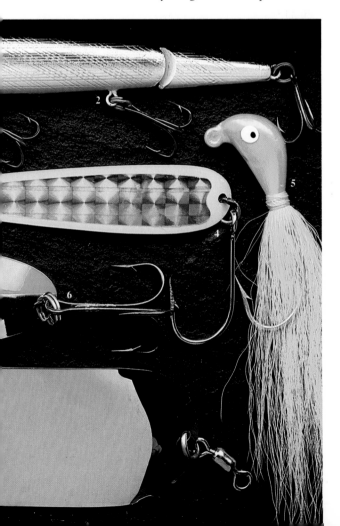

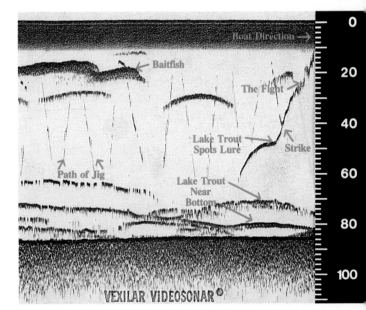

VERTICAL JIGGING works best with a lead-head jig or vibrating blade. Simply lower the lure to the bottom; then reel it back rapidly. This graph tape shows a laker striking a jig as it falls.

LAKE TROUT lures include (1) Sonar, (2) jointed Rebel, (3) Rapala, (4) Flutter Spoon, (5) bucktail, (6) Little Cleo spoon, (7) Dodger/fly combination.

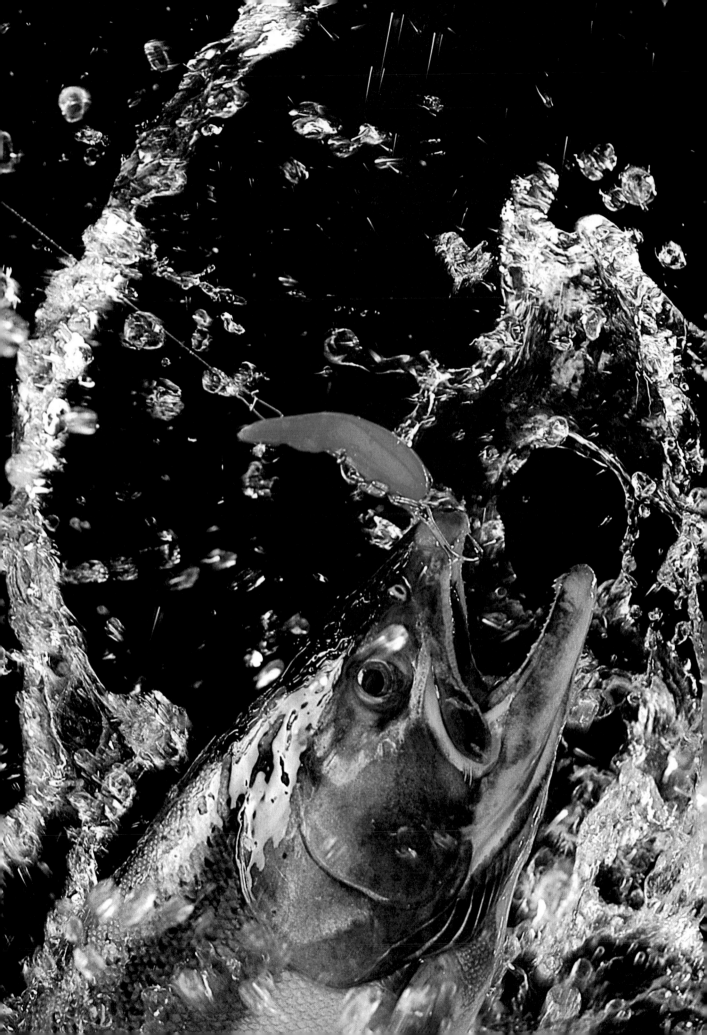

Pacific Salmon

For centuries, salmon have mystified man by their uncanny ability to cross thousands of miles of open sea, and return to spawn in the streams where their lives began. Because of their tremendous stamina and speed, salmon rank as the ultimate sport fishing prize among many fishermen.

Five species of salmon are native to the Pacific Coast of North America: chinook, coho, pink, sockeye and chum. Chinook and coho, largest of the Pacific salmon, are the favorites of fishermen.

For many years, fisheries agencies tried to stock salmon in freshwater lakes. Most of these efforts failed. Then, in 1966, coho salmon were introduced in Lake Michigan in an attempt to control the lake's huge population of alewives and to create a new sport fishery. The salmon thrived on the small baitfish. In 1967 and 1968, salmon weighing 7 to 17 pounds returned to the streams where they were stocked, signalling the beginning of a sport fishing bonanza. The project's success led to more coho stocking and later, to the introduction of chinooks. Today, Lakes Michigan and Huron support thriving salmon fisheries, while some fish are taken in Superior, Erie and Ontario.

In the Great Lakes, chinook and cohos feed on alewives, smelt and chubs. They also eat insects and crustaceans. The salmon grow at an astounding rate. Chinooks commonly reach 30 pounds over a normal 4-year life span. Sea-run salmon gain weight even faster, sometimes exceeding 50 pounds.

Salmon need cold water to survive, preferring temperatures about 55°F. They are seldom caught where the temperature is more than a few degrees from that mark. In the Great Lakes, winds and currents move huge masses of water, causing drastic temperature changes over short periods of time. Salmon detect these fluctuations and follow water of their preferred temperature. As a result, salmon may be near the shore one day and miles from shore the next. Or, they can be schooling on the surface at sunrise and lying in 100-foot depths in the afternoon.

Salmon are *anadromous* fish, which means they spend their adult lives in the sea, then return to freshwater streams to spawn. Barriers such as low dams and waterfalls cannot keep them from reaching their spawning grounds. They are powerful swimmers, capable of hurdling rapids and falls that would seem impossible to ascend.

Salmon in the Great Lakes spend their entire lives in fresh water. The vast open waters of the Great Lakes serve as their ocean and the tributary streams are their spawning grounds. Although some spawn successfully, not enough young are produced to maintain a quality fishery. So, state fisheries crews trap the returning salmon, remove their eggs and rear the fish in hatcheries. Then, the young salmon are released in streams. Unlike most fish, Pacific salmon have a set life span. Most individuals of the same species return to spawn at the same age, and then die.

Pacific Salmon
Combined Range

CHINOOK or king salmon are the largest of the Pacific salmon. Their life span is four years, though a few live five or six years. When hooked, a chinook may run 200 yards or more. Many a fisherman has watched awestruck and helpless as the line disappears from the reel. After the first run, a chinook usually fights deep and rarely jumps. The world-record chinook, 92 pounds, was caught in the Skeena River, British Columbia in 1959.

COHO, or silver salmon do not grow as large as chinooks, although many anglers regard cohos as the sportiest of the salmon. They jump repeatedly and change direction so quickly the angler mistakenly believes the fish has broken free. Cohos usually live only three years, gaining much of their weight in the last few months of life. The world-record coho, 31 pounds, was caught in Cowichan Bay, British Columbia in 1947.

How to Identify Chinook and Coho

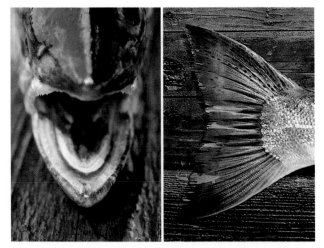

CHINOOKS have a lower jaw that comes to a sharp point. The inside of the mouth appears dusky gray or black and the teeth are set in black gums. The anal fin, the bottom fin closest to the tail, usually has 15 to 19 rays. The tail is broad and covered with spots.

COHOS have a lower jaw that appears more blunt than that of the chinook. The inside of the mouth is dusky gray or black, but the teeth are set in white gums. The anal fin is shorter, with only 12 to 15 rays. The tail may have no spots or just a few on the upper portion.

When and Where to Catch Salmon

Adult salmon rely on cover and structure less than other fish. They go where they must to find food and a comfortable water temperature.

In the Great Lakes, salmon schools are scattered during spring and early summer. Their search for 53° to 57°F temperatures may take them miles from shore or within casting distance of piers. Although fishing is excellent on some days, catching salmon consistently is difficult. But as spawning time nears, they gather near tributary streams where finding and catching them becomes easier.

OPEN-WATER fishing accounts for most salmon caught in the Great Lakes. Salmon have seasonal migration patterns in each lake, so anglers should check with local sources as to the location of fish as the season progresses.

STREAM FISHING for salmon in Great Lakes tributaries begins in September and continues into October. Along the Pacific Coast, some salmon enter streams in April, though most runs begin in September.

Factors Affecting Water Temperature

STREAM MOUTHS attract salmon, especially when surrounding water is too cold. Salmon move into the warm-water plume created by the stream to find suitable temperatures.

DISCHARGES from power plants draw in salmon when lakes are cold. Though the discharged water is too warm, it mixes with lake water, creating a zone of ideal temperature.

WINDS force salmon to move so they can stay at the right temperature. On-shore winds hold warm water along shore; offshore winds push it out and cold water wells up to replace it.

Trolling: Hunting Big Water for Salmon

Trolling enables anglers to cover large areas in a short time, increasing their chances of finding salmon that are scattered in open water. Most trollers use several lines, so they can experiment with different lures and depths to find the combination that best fits the situation at hand.

Of course, it is possible to catch salmon simply by running a line behind the boat and trolling at random. But specialized equipment, such as a temperature gauge, recording sonar unit, downriggers and trolling boards, greatly improves the odds of finding and catching salmon.

A DOWNRIGGER consists of a large reel filled with steel cable, a crank and a brake to keep the reel from slipping. Some have a built-in rod holder and a counter to record the depth of the *cannonball*.

DOWNRIGGERS permit fishing in deep water with relatively light tackle. A 15- to 20-pound test line is attached to a release mechanism (inset) on the weight or cannonball, which is lowered on a cable to the desired depth. A striking salmon will jerk the line loose, so the angler can fight the fish on a free line. Two lines can be used with a *stacker*. This is a release device attached to the cable, rather than to the cannonball. Most salmon boats have at least two downriggers; many have four. Thus, as many as eight lines can be trolled at once.

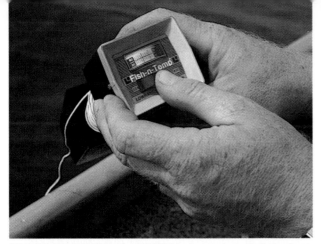

TEMPERATURE GAUGES help anglers find the best fishing depth. The probe is lowered until it reaches the salmon's preferred temperature range. Some trolling boats have built-in surface temperature gauges.

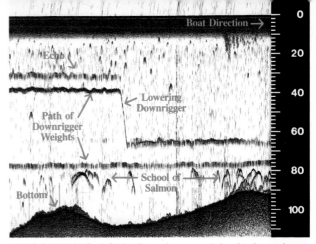

RECORDING SONAR units reveal both the salmon and the paths of downrigger weights. As salmon change depth, the location of the cannonball is adjusted so the lures run just above the fish.

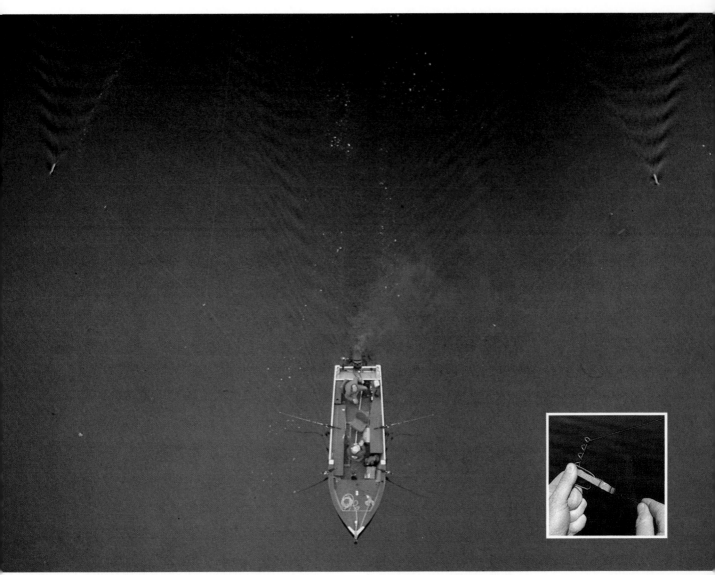

TROLLING BOARDS keep lines wide of the boat when fishing shallow water. Salmon are extremely boat-shy, so drawing the lines away from the wake reduces the chance of spooking fish near the surface. The boards are pulled by cords attached to a pole in the boat. They plane 50 to 75 feet to the side. Fishing lines are attached to release devices (inset) that slide down the cords toward the trolling boards. Two lines can be fished off each side of the boat. With lines spread 20 to 30 feet apart, the fisherman can cover a wide swath of water.

Shore Casting:
Try Spoons and Spawn Bags

Shore fishermen begin catching salmon in early summer, months before the spawning run begins. Salmon stay in the vicinity of stream mouths, generally feeding just off shore for a few hours in early morning. During midday, they move miles from shore, but return again in evening.

Most fishermen cast with flashy spoons. Heavy lures are best, because they can be cast farther. Still-fishing with spawn bags and alewives also works well. A heavy-duty spinning rod and a large spinning reel with at least 250 yards of 20-pound test monofilament are ideal for shore casting.

ROCKY POINTS near stream mouths are schooling sites for salmon prior to spawning. They often porpoise on the surface in early morning and late afternoon, when they are caught by shore casters.

STREAM-MOUTH fishermen wear chest waders to reach salmon beyond casting distance from shore. To keep the surf from topping their waders, they wear raincoats with belts snug around the waist.

Pier Fishing:
A Way to Work Deep Water from Shore

Piers, especially those near stream mouths, attract salmon throughout the year. However, the best fishing is just before the spawning run or after the run has started. Piers are popular because they enable anglers to fish deep water that could not be reached from shore.

PIER fishermen use the same tackle and lures as shore casters. However, a long-handled landing net and a long stringer are helpful, because most piers stand high above the water surface.

Stream Fishing:
Look for Beds and Barriers

Even before salmon begin their upstream migrations, they begin changing from bright silver to dark brown and finally to black. Their digestive tracts shrink to almost nothing and they stop eating. As a result, salmon are reluctant to bite once they move into their home streams. Still, many are taken during the spawning run, probably because they strike out of instinct rather than hunger.

At the spawning sites, female salmon dig shallow nests or *redds* on the stream bottom. Once on their redds, salmon spook easily and are difficult to catch. Some anglers spend hours fishing the same redd.

DAMS AND WATERFALLS block or slow migrating salmon. Fish collect in downstream pools, where they are caught by casting spoons, spinners or jigs. Salmon in swifter current may be taken by drift-fishing (page 138).

DRIFT BOATS carry salmon fishermen down many Pacific Coast streams. The boat's swept-up ends make them safe in strong rapids. One person maneuvers the boat with oars, while another angler casts from the bow.

SPAWNING STREAMS become jammed with salmon during the run. As spawning time nears, male salmon develop a grotesque appearance. At right center in the photo is a hooked-jawed male; below it, a female.

Natural Bait: The Old Reliable

Natural baits are used extensively by West Coast salmon fishermen and are becoming more popular on the Great Lakes. Favorite baits include alewives, smelt, herring and fresh spawn.

Trolling, still-fishing or *mooching* are common bait-fishing techniques. When mooching, the angler drops the bait to the bottom, then slowly raises and lowers the bait while the boat drifts. When fishing with fresh spawn, most anglers still-fish or drift-fish with a single egg, a gob of eggs or a spawn bag.

FRESH BAITFISH look more natural and stay on the hook better than frozen bait. Fishermen can catch their own bait around piers, harbors or warmwater discharges with umbrella nets (above), dip nets or cast nets.

LIVE FISH are rigged on a harness with a #4 single hook and a #6 treble hook as a trailer. Insert the first hook through the lips or nostrils and the trailer hook under the skin, just behind the dorsal fin.

How to Tie a Spawn Bag

A SPAWN BAG is made with a 2-inch square piece of nylon cut from a roll of mesh or a nylon stocking.

WRAP the eggs to form a bag about one-half inch in diameter. Tie it with thread and trim the excess material.

INSERT a #4 or #6 hook securely into the spawn bag. It should be well concealed in the bag.

Artificial Lures:
Bright Colors and Flashy Action

Salmon like colorful, flashy lures with a lot of action. Color of the lure depends on weather, location and season. In general, chartreuse, green, blue and silver lures work best. Red and orange lures often catch salmon just before spawning time.

Silvery colors are the best choice on sunny days; fluorescent or phosphorescent colors on cloudy days. Some fishermen flash their phosphorescent lures with a lantern or camera strobe to make them glow in the water.

DODGERS are large metal attractors that are attached ahead of a thin spoon, small plug or trolling fly. The added flash and action, as seen in this multiple-exposure photograph, entices salmon to strike.

LURES for chinook and coho salmon include (1) Tad-polly, (2) Krocodile, (3) Little Cleo spoon, (4) trolling squid, (5) trolling fly, (6) Fireplug, (7) Flatfish, (8) J-Plug, (9) Rebel, (10) Flutter Spoon.

Index